Language and Literacies

Selected papers from the
Annual Meeting of the British Association for Applied Linguistics
held at the University of Manchester, September 1998

Edited by
Teresa O'Brien

Advisory Board: Srikant Sarangi, Gunther Kress, Celia Roberts

BRITISH ASSOCIATION FOR APPLIED LINGUISTICS
in association with
MULTILINGUAL MATTERS LTD
Clevedon • Buffalo • Toronto • Sydney

British Library Cataloguing in Publication Data

A CIP catalogue record for this book is available from the British Library.

ISBN 1-85359-486-5 (pbk)

Multilingual Matters Ltd
UK: Frankfurt Lodge, Clevedon Hall, Victoria Road, Clevedon, England BS21 7HH.
USA: UTP, 2250 Military Road, Tonawanda, NY 14150, USA.
Canada: UTP, 5201 Dufferin Street, North York, Ontario, M3H 5T8, Canada.
Australia: PO Box 586, Artamon NSW 2064, Australia.

Copyright © 1999 Teresa O'Brien and the authors of the individual chapters.

Typeset by Wayside Books, Clevedon.
Printed and bound in Great Britain by Short Run Press Ltd.

Contents

Introduction: The pluralisation of literacy

TERESA O'BRIEN
University of Manchester

The theme chosen for the 31st BAAL Annual Meeting, held in September 1998 at the University of Manchester, was *Language and Literacies*.[1] This brief introduction to selected papers from the Meeting situates them with reference to important points of focus in contemporary literacy studies.

The early eighties saw the publication of several works which laid the foundations for what has become in the nineties a widening and deepening of interest in the social contexts in which literacy practices and events occur. The influence of the ethnographic work of Heath (1983) and Street (1984), among others, is acknowledged in the majority of contemporary literacy studies. Heath's study of situated literacy practices in two different US communities and in their schools gave many of us a first sense of plurality. Street gave us the distinction between an *ideological* approach, which accepts that what is meant by literacy varies from situation to situation and is dependent on ideology, and *autonomous* approaches which claim that literacy can be defined separately from the social context. Barton (1994: 38), adopting an ideological approach, speaks of a literacy as 'a stable, coherent, identifiable configuration of practices' and points out that 'people have different literacies which they make use of, associated with different domains of life'. He has worked with other colleagues (e.g. Barton & Ivanic, 1991) to raise the profile of the study of 'everyday', as opposed to academic literacy, particularly that of adults. Baynham's case studies of Moroccans in London (1995) also focus on everyday literacy events, highlighting the complexity and richness of working with the literacy practices of two languages – another important plurality. This, at primary school level, is also the concern of Gregory (1996) in her work with bilingual children and their families. Several studies in Hasan & Williams (1996) look at the different literacies involved in areas of the curriculum: reading geography is not the same as reading history. Hasan (1996) distinguishes between the necessary but limiting *recognition literacy* and *action literacy* which is linked with an informed genre-based pedagogy. Her methods are different from Heath's but the concern that all children should have access to the literacies they need is the same. We can speak, too, of gendered literacies as illustrated, for example, by Rockhill (1993) and to some extent by Kalaja & Pitkänen Huhta, and Zubair in this volume. Freire has inspired work on critical literacy (Freire & Macedo, 1987) exemplified here by Cook and O'Halloran, and by Wallace.

Thus far, literacy has been assumed to mean primarily print literacy. But, as Barton (1994: 13) points out, the term *literacy* has become a metaphor applied to other areas, e.g. computer literacy, media literacy and visual literacy. All of these were the focus of papers at the Annual Meeting: van Leeuwen discussed the literacy of *guide interfaces* which allow CD-Rom users to navigate a database; Richardson considered the consequences for media literacy of the new viewing position in the age of satellite, cable and digital transmission when the position of the national viewer is no longer relevant; Meinhof explored similar issues in the context of an eastern German region and these themes are followed up in Richardson & Meinhof (1999). Kress & van Leeuwen (1996) have addressed visual literacy and Kress pursues the theme in this volume and raises interesting questions about the boundaries of applied linguistics. While not comprehensive, this brief survey suggests why it has become necessary to pluralise literacy. The papers in the volume bear witness, we hope, to the value of a multi-literacy approach.

It was to be expected that the world of education would be strongly represented at Manchester and it does indeed provide the context for the majority of the papers. The selection begins with a series of reactions to the National Literacy Strategy (NLS) – an innovation in the primary schools of England and Wales. It then moves through several other papers which explore aspects of the world of formal education in various parts of the world. These are arranged in ascending order, beginning with papers focused on primary education in Britain, moving on to secondary school children in Chile (L1 home literacy practices) and Finland (L2), and then to further and tertiary education in Britain (L1 and L2). The remaining papers deal with the wider world, although many carry implications for educational policy and practice. One of the issues discussed in the paper on contrastive rhetoric is that of *norms and conventions*, and this is then taken up specifically in the next paper on the reform of German orthography. A rural community in the developing world is the context for a consideration of gendered literacy. The last two papers are thematically linked: they both highlight the increasing interaction between image and linguistic text that characterises modern communication. Both look at texts intended for the general public and demonstrate the importance of being literate across both semiotic systems. The papers move then from school to the wider community; from approaches that are largely linguistic to those which include other ways of meaning and which point forward to the inevitable changes in the communicational landscape.

In summaries of their presentations for the colloquium on the NLS, Bourne, Kress, Street and Sealey provide a variety of perspectives on the early Framework within a broadly welcoming, though not uncritical, stance. Bourne argues from her research experience of multi-ethnic schools that schools and teachers with shared aims and consistent strategies can make a difference and welcomes the explicit nature of the NLS. She also sees the strategy as part of a multi-agency approach and wills it to work. Kress also wants to be supportive; he discusses the politics, the resources and the understandings necessary to make it work. He suggests also that the extension of the strategy to secondary schools may have positive cross-curricular effects but predicts a crisis for English as a subject. Street is directly critical of the very narrow conception of literacy which he identifies as firmly rooted in an autonomous model of literacy in which there is little attention to contexts, to contrasts between home and school as sites of social practice, or to the relation between home and school with respect to literacy learning. Sealey recognises the positive aspects of the strategy but is concerned about the theory of language implied by a strategy which has omitted useful conceptual tools such as *discourse, register* and *semantic field*. The overall supportive tone of the colloquium is aided by a postscript on later developments which tells of productive meetings between those responsible for the NLS and representatives of BAAL and the Linguistics Association of Great Britain.

One of the early concerns expressed by applied linguists at the introduction of the NLS was the apparent neglect of the needs of those pupils for whom English is an additional language. Although not directly addressing the NLS, Gardner and Rea-Dickins focus on the related matter of assessment of literacy and oracy and take issue with a document from the Office of Standards in Education (OFSTED) which has suggested the abandonment of English Language Stages as created and used by language support teachers. They present an interesting argument for their retention which views the Stages as valuable texts embodying important practices which result from the expertise of their users.

Moving into secondary education, away from Britain and into another language, Gibbons, Lascar and Morales explore the role of social class and home literacy practices in the literacy proficiency of Chilean adolescents. While reasserting the value of home reading found in other studies (Wells, 1985), the findings throw doubt on any direct linkage between socio-economic status and literacy and the authors suggest that some problems of children from lower socio-economic backgrounds may be rooted in stereotypes and attitudes, rather than substantive differences in behaviour. The paper includes an interesting example of the way register operates in Spanish textbooks written for primary and secondary schools. The methodology of the survey of literacy practices was developed with help from Wells of the Ontario Institute for Studies in Education and the paper would provide a useful model for others working in Spanish-speaking environments.

Kalaja and Pitkänen-Huhta focus on an EFL secondary classroom in Finland where they uncover two different literacies at work: that of the teacher and that of some of the pupils (the boys). Foreign language teachers will probably recognise the scenario described but might not have conceptualised the events in quite the same way. The teacher-imposed literacy revealed through the transcript stresses a superficial processing of the text and the completion of the school task in a fast and efficient way. The student-imposed literacy is constructed through talk *around* text which resists the superficial and efficient completion of the task and might involve joking and playing with words. The students would rather see the task as meaningful group effort related to their world. Although the writers mention that it is the boys who impose their own literacy, they do not develop the gendered aspect of what they have observed. There is clearly further work to be done here.

There are links to be made between the Finnish paper and that of Wallace. Both deal with L2 literacy and reading as a social process; both look at *talk about text*. In both, we see teachers working to an agenda which is not the same as their students' and we are led, through careful analysis of language and context, to see the ways in which teachers, while intending to facilitate their students' learning, do not always do so.

Wallace's main concern is the development of critical literacy skills in an advanced and motivated EFL class taught by herself. (The texts studied are from newspapers, texts which integrate words with pictures and typographical features to convey meanings.) She distinguishes her approach to teaching critical literacy from approaches which emphasise personal development and involvement and encourage the equal valuing of diverse cultural practices. Rejecting this relativist position, she aims to encourage the achievement of distance in her students so that they are prepared, if necessary, to censure practices typical of a cultural milieu, their own or that of others. Her treatment of the data related to her own practice illustrates this distance and provides a useful example of both linguistic and practitioner research. In a series of extracts from transcripts, Wallace shows herself gradually relaxing the control that she exercises over the students' responses in order to allow them to articulate the critical responses they are capable of.

The next paper takes us into the area of writing studies. Lillis, like Wallace, uses her own practice as she demonstrates from supervision transcripts that also include *talk about text* the tension that 'non-traditional' student-writers in Higher Education often experience between what they feel they want to say and what they feel they are allowed to say in their academic writing. Drawing on and connecting ideas from Ivanic (1998), Clark & Ivanic (1997) and Fairclough (1992), and on Bakhtin's notion of addressivity, Lillis creates an effective heuristic for exploring student meaning-making. A subtle analysis of two students' views of their relationship to their writing and to academia avoids a straightforward dichotomy between the personal and the institutional and shows how personal interest is bound up with dominant ways of meaning in Higher Education.

Connor deals with the study of writing across languages and gives an overview of her field showing how the developing concepts of genre and culture have been integrated to create a modern contrastive rhetoric. She signals further developments in the complex area of norms and standards of writing as we move towards something called *Eurorhetoric* which, she suggests, is emerging from the intermingling of readers and writers of different linguistic backgrounds in considering, for instance, grant proposals for EU funding written in English.

In her very informative paper, Johnson gives us an insight into a current example of norm development. Teachers of German will be grateful for the clear detailing of the principal features of recent reform in German orthography and students of language standardisation will appreciate the account and analysis of the dispute which has ensued from the reform and which has gone rather further than complaints in the press.

Bringing us back to our theme of literacies, Zubair in a paper on work in progress in a rural Pakistani community shows how intergenerational changes are taking place in women's literacy use. She plots the gendering of literacy practices in terms of literacy events and languages. Using transcripts of focus groups she shows that younger women are no longer re-enacting the roles of *silent* and *caged birds* and are ready to challenge the existing concepts of women's literacy. She reminds us how the development of other people's literacy can be viewed as threatening to those who hold power.

Opening up new ground for applied linguists, Kress gives an overview of the meanings that were the concern of the meeting and suggests a new agenda. It is perhaps worth noting the gap that exists between this agenda and the political agenda embodied in the National Literacy Strategy. The paper focuses on the challenges facing those with an interest in literacy, whether the focus be social, technological, cultural, economic, representational, or theoretical. Kress is concerned to move away from the fragmentation of knowledge and understanding which so often results from the separatist organisation of academic life and to work instead towards the possibility of integration. He deals specifically with two issues: theoretical divergences with the ensuing problems; and the changing 'real world' of representation. An important argument is that changes in the communicational landscape are leading us away from the study of language alone towards study of the relations between language and image and of their respective semiotic functions.

Cook and O'Halloran share this broader aspiration for applied linguistics. They exemplify the approach that Kress advocates in their investigation of the design and accessibility of baby-food labels. Their study points to the social importance of analyses of widely distributed texts of public significance and of the dissemination of the findings of such analyses. In particular, they examine the assumptions made by legislators and the food industry about readers, meaning and the nature of interpretation. For those who might be considering such work, the paper provides an excellent, detailed example of an analysis of multi-functional text combining linguistics with paralinguistic resources and implicitly indicates the skills that will need to be developed if people are to reach 'the state of being comfortable inside a sign-sharing community' (Jennings & Purves, 1991: 3).

Whilst I have tried to draw attention to some of the links which exist between the papers, it is clear that there are far more to be made as readers draw on their own literacies to interpret and find value in them.

Acknowledgements

I would like to thank the BAAL Advisory Board (Srikant Sarangi, Gunther Kress and Celia Roberts) and Susan Hunston for assistance in editing this volume.

Note

1. When the theme was announced at the 30th Annual Meeting in 1997, I overheard a colleague wondering why *literacy* had been pluralised. It was our hope that the meeting would place the plural form firmly in the lexicon of all our members and that the papers would demonstrate the variety of literacies which exists to be studied. Although we have not been able to represent the full range in this volume, this hope was largely realised at the Meeting.

References

Barton, D. (1994) *Literacy: An Introduction to the Ecology of Written Language*. Oxford: Blackwell.
Barton, D. and Ivanic, R. (eds) (1991) *Writing in the Community*. London: Sage.
Baynham, M. (1995) *Literacy Practices*. London and New York: Longman.
Clark, R. and Ivanic, R. (1997) *The Politics of Writing*. London: Routledge.
Fairclough, N. (1992) *Discourse and Social Change*. Cambridge: Polity Press.

Freire, P. and Macedo, D. (1987) *Literacy: Reading the word and the world.* London: Routledge.

Gregory, E. (1996) *Making Sense of a New World.* Liverpool: Paul Chapman Publishing.

Hasan, R. (1986) Literacy, everyday talk and society. In R. Hasan and G. Williams (eds) *Literacy in Society.* London and New York: Longman.

Hasan, R. and Williams, G. (eds) (1996) *Literacy in Society.* London and New York: Longman.

Heath, S. B. (1983) *Ways with Words.* Cambridge: Cambridge University Press.

Ivanic, R. (1998) *Writing and Identity: The discoursal construction of identity in academic writing.* Amsterdam: Benjamins.

Jennings, E. M. and Purves, A. C. (eds) (1991) *Literate Systems and Individual Lives: Perspectives on literacy and schooling.* New York: State University of New York Press.

Kress, G. and van Leeuwen, T. (1996) *Reading Images.* London: Routledge.

Richardson, K. and Meinhof, U. (1999) *Worlds in Common?* London: Routledge.

Rockhill, K. (1993) Gender, language and the politics of literacy. In B. Street (ed.) *Cross-cultural Approaches to Literacy.* Cambridge: Cambridge University Press.

Street, B. (1984) *Literacy in Theory and Practice.* Cambridge: Cambridge University Press.

Wells, G. (ed.) (1985) *Language, Learning and Education: Selected papers from the Bristol study, language at home and at school.* Windsor, Berks: NFER Nelson.

1 The National Literacy Strategy: A debate

JILL BOURNE
University of Southampton

GUNTHER KRESS
Institute of Education, University of London

BRIAN STREET
King's College, University of London

ALISON SEALEY
University of Warwick

Abstract

The colloquium on the newly introduced National Literacy Strategy included short presentations from four speakers. Each took a slightly different perspective, and these are reflected in the written summaries of their presentations which are included here. While there is a large measure of support for the Strategy, there are important points to be addressed.

Intervening to Raise Attainment in Schools
JILL BOURNE

Introduction: What is the National Literacy Strategy?

Within a year of coming into office, the New Labour government launched a National Literacy Strategy (DfEE, 1998)[1] as a part of its programme towards fulfilling its electoral commitments to the education of all children in school.

---

[1]See Appendix for glossary of acronyms.

The explicit aim of the National Literacy Strategy (NLS) is to improve educational outcomes for all pupils and do away with the long tail of underachievement which has dogged the English education system. It aims to raise overall standards of attainment by raising the standards of literacy in primary schools over five years. The high profile nature of this initiative is illustrated by the promise of the Secretary of State for Education, David Blunkett, to resign if the targets he has set for improving literacy levels have not been met by 2002.

The NLS provides a framework of teaching objectives term by term for each year of schooling for children from five to 11 years. The framework analyses its teaching objectives as consisting of three interweaving strands: focusing on language at word (sounds, spelling and vocabulary), sentence (grammatical knowledge and punctuation) and text (comprehension and composition) levels. Word, sentence and text level objectives are intended to be studied in parallel, and wherever possible in context, in each term and for every age range.

As well as teaching objectives, the framework provides a firm structure of time and class management. It thus gives details both of what should be taught and the means by which it should be taught. Fundamental to the Strategy is 'a daily period of dedicated literacy teaching time for all pupils'. It includes the reading and discussion of texts, and shared writing, where the teacher models and discusses the writing process of different genres with the class. It also requires teachers to include 15 minutes of focused word and/or sentence level study each day.

Now, I (like many colleagues) feel there are areas of the Framework which I would like to amend, alter, or develop more fully. However, I want to argue that BAAL should be seen to be actively supporting the NLS aims to address widening access to literacy, and to do this we need to negotiate useful amendments in a constructive manner, working with the Strategy, rather than loftily criticising its academic limitations, or attempting to undermine it. As Lyotard (1984: 50) has argued:

> The moment knowledge ceases to be an end in itself ... its transmission is no longer the exclusive responsibility of scholars and students. The notion of 'university franchise' belongs to a bygone era.

Today academics must work alongside a range of other areas of interest in the public arena, or stand marginalised and ignored. Applied Linguists, perhaps more than many academics, should welcome this.

Why I Support the NLS

I support the changes in policy underlying the introduction of the NLS because it is firmly based on the principle that the underachievement of children in schools is not simply due to differences in the innate abilities of young people. Underachievement in schools is seen as playing an important part in the process of naturalising differential access to wealth and social exclusion. The long tail of underperformance of (mainly poor) children has at last come to be seen as simply unacceptable. Schools and teachers, working together with shared aims and consistent strategies, can make a difference. I personally found evidence for this in the recent study for the DFEE on teaching and learning strategies in successful multi-ethnic schools (Blair & Bourne, 1998). There, highly successful schools were identified which were meeting the needs of all children, monitoring progress carefully, by gender, ethnicity and crude indicators of poverty (numbers of children eligible for free school meals), and targeting support to lessen differentials between groups, as well as to raise the achievement of individual pupils.

Within the National Literacy Strategy Framework, the curriculum is both explicit and publicly available term by term and year by year. In this way, it has the potential to weaken the external boundaries between home and school (and indeed school and teacher training institutions). It does this firstly by making school practices transparent and open to parents (and students). Secondly, it aims to give all children access to a wide range of written texts, modelling the different reading and writing strategies involved, while allowing for differential rates of progress and different levels of support through group and individual work. Thirdly, it weakens boundaries by deliberately siting its activities in the popular sphere, by broadcasting its aims and its methods.

Multi-agency Approaches

This fits within wider initiatives such as the National Childcare Strategy, focused on developing local partnerships to plan provision across the board for children 0–14 years old, bringing teachers into working groups with social workers, child care workers, youth workers, librarians, housing department officials and health visitors, to thrash out integrated approaches for the welfare of children. Funding has been set aside to meet successful bids for local programmes implementing government backed initiatives involving parents and children together: such as homework clubs, summer study centres, and family literacy initiatives. These 'joined up' interventions suggest the need for a more explicit, shared curriculum, so different groups can work together in different sites.

The explicit nature of the NLS Framework means that both children themselves and their parents are encouraged to be aware of and play a part in discussing the progress and setting targets for each child. Target setting and assessment methods are now being developed by teachers which are inclusive of all children, and which involve the children explicitly in their own target setting and assessment process from a young age, so they know what teachers are aiming for and can consider their own progress, preferences and successes.

A New Teacher Training Curriculum

At the same time as the launch of the NLS in schools, a new national curriculum for initial teacher training came into force (DfEE Circular, 4/98). Within this document, which appears to have been created by, or with strong input from, those responsible for developing the NLS, the content of what all new teachers need to know in order to be able to teach the Literacy Hour to the national literacy framework is set out explicitly. While many teacher educators may grieve for the loss of autonomy in planning courses, the ITT curriculum alongside the NLS Framework offer opportunities for creating shared understandings between schools and teacher training institutions. For the first time, beginning teachers and their placement schools have a shared language to talk about practice. For the first time, teacher educators can predict the contexts into which their students will be going on school placement, and plan to give them the knowledge and understanding of language and literacy they will need to make the literacy strategy work within the classroom. In 1998/9, students were privileged – all schools this year were involved in NLS training. This meant access to lots of debate in staffrooms on strategies and practice. The students I work with have benefited enormously from joining school inservice training sessions, and taking part in discussions on principles and practice in the staffroom.

Conclusion

I want the programme to work. I want language study to be 'popular'; I want there to be a shared language for talking about language which is not elitist, but which focuses on ways of analysing language which help people do what they want to do with language, or do it better (that is, a functional model of language). The first NLS Framework offers a high profile start, offering applied linguists a point of intervention. Involvement in the development of supportive materials and supportive teacher education materials to enable the Strategy to work as effectively as possible would be one positive way forward. Another would be the co-operative and supportive development of the Framework in co-operation with the NLS team, as an evolving process with a shared goal: greater access to literacy and wider educational success for all. Existing expertise on how language works is obviously going to be useful in transforming educational approaches, but only if we are willing to work with other forms of knowledge and expertise: on teaching and learning, on child care, on health and housing, on employment strategies, and on all the other forces which combine to enhance or deny opportunities for educational success in our society. In this new context of multi-agency approaches to change, I feel we should step with some humility.

The NLS: Making it Work in Primary and Secondary Schools

GUNTHER KRESS

Why I Support the NLS

The introduction of the NLS poses a severe challenge to a professional association such as BAAL and its members; in other words, to me, to all of us. The challenge consists in two things: one, in overcoming the traditional academic response to changes in the world, which is to analyse and to provide critique; and two, to resist the temptation to engage with the politics of the NLS on a political level. Both prove just about impossible for the traditional academic, and I include myself in that category. On both counts, there is plenty to have misgivings about; I will try to set an example here by not offering a single critical comment.

My reason for supporting the NLS comes from a recognition of a near catastrophic and nearly utter absence of knowledge relevant to certain forms of successful teaching around the issue of literacy. This is not a critique of teachers' professional competence, nor of the insight that they have gained in their professional lives, nor a critique of their pedagogic knowledge around strategies that help. It is a comment on nearly two generations' worth not just of neglect of concern with formal knowledge about language, but of a still persistent view in some quarters, a still settled view that such knowledge was detrimental to the development of creativity. This had produced, by the early 1980s, when I encountered these views in Australia, the obverse of what had in the 1960s been a revolutionary move in English teaching. It is, on my part, a critique of those academics whose task it should have been to play their role in renewing the profession theoretically, and who instead took pride in intellectual complacency about a 'tradition' that had to be defended. If in this I sound like certain critics from the former right or from the present political establishment then I think that I differ from them in that I do not see the problem as 'filling their heads with useless theory', but rather that I think some academics have been at fault, in a near scandalous fashion, in not providing knowledge, whether in Teacher Education or in In service courses of a kind which actually enhances the skills base of teachers in this respect. There is, as a consequence, a chasm of ignorance of any formal knowledge about language.

In this context, yet more critique of an initiative such as the NLS is precisely what is not needed. This is particularly so as teachers themselves are in my experience very much aware – and worried about – that lack of knowledge and are very keen to do all in their power to amend that. There is a noticeable charge, a level of energy, of commitment; and I see it as my task to do what I can to play my part in making relevant knowledge available in useful form.

What Will it Need for the NLS to Work?

(a) The 'politics' in the school, and in the profession

It is a very great pity that this government, like the last, has continued by and large to pursue punitive means ('blame and shame'), rather than a policy of support, encouragement, and reward. In the school it is essential now that on the one hand the aim to increase competence in this area is taken on as a responsibility by the whole school, rather than as a responsibility handed to some individuals, or, in the secondary school to a particular department. In the primary school it is of course much easier to involve every teacher. But parents and governors also need to be fully involved. And in the secondary school it is essential that all teachers understand – even recognising that the Technology teacher has never had any (need for) such training before – that it is a task for each and every teacher and every department or faculty.

(b) The resources

The most crucial resource is that of knowledge. In its absence among staff, money is the seemingly obvious means to supply this shortfall. This is where an association such as BAAL and all of its members have a crucial role: this organisation has relevant knowledge for in service courses and for the production of materials. The current huge popularity of materials – just ANY materials – from Australia speaks volumes in this context. In Australia, as most of us are aware, work of this kind has been going on for some 15 years, though even with such a vast lead-time there is, even in Australia, a dearth of trainers and of materials.

(c) The understanding of language and communication

In the absence of an involvement by an association such as BAAL and of its members, the tried and tested 'bootstrap' method will be – and is now – being applied. The fact that it has failed each of its tests will not prevent its renewed application. On the government's side – and that of its quangos (TTA, CAA, the Inspectorate, etc.) it means a likely falling back on older models, older forms of grammar, or, equally problematic, on certain contemporary mainstream forms of linguistics; on the school's side it means harnessing what is insufficient theory and knowledge existent in schools. Often it will mean, as the obvious solution, asking the English department to be responsible. But English, as I said at the beginning, does not necessarily have these knowledges available, simply qua English.

The older understandings of language and of communication will not suffice to support a real attempt to bring the skills and knowledge base of the profession up to what is required. What is required is a commitment by the government over the medium to long term (i.e. a 5 to 10-year programme; of course with such measures as can be taken in the meantime).

What Effects Will the NLS Have on the Curriculum, and on English in Particular?

It seems likely that the NLS – in some form – will be extended into secondary schools; and even now many schools are taking measures which in some way or other anticipate some such project. There will, as far as I can see, be significant effects on the curriculum overall. The strategy will, if it is to be in any way serious and effective, have to work across all curriculum subjects. This will break down the insulation between subject-areas on the one hand, and it will have – even if not in the short term – effects on the curricular content of all subjects, as it will on their aims and effects.

The most serious question will be posed for the school subject English. In as far as its integrative and cohesive principles are even now exceedingly weak and weakening further, the removal of the presently perhaps central content and goal of communication, and its dispersal (or integrated imposition) across all subjects in the secondary school, will leave English in the severest crisis. As a school-subject it will continue to exist – the politics of removing it are at this time too serious in their repercussion – yet it will exist in a context where its central plank has been removed.

Conclusion

As always, the response open to academics is as I said that of critique; there is more than enough scope for that. Withholding support is a 'safe bet': if the NLS collapses, the response will be seen to have been justified; and without real support it is unlikely to succeed beyond a limited extent. However an absolutely essential opportunity to apply, in a real sense, the knowledge lodged in members of this Association will have been lost. A disabling knowledge-deficit will remain, to the medium and long term detriment of education, of children in schools, and of this society. Notions of equity and of social responsibility demand, in my view, full support at this point in educational politics.

The NLS: Some theoretical and textual Considerations
BRIAN STREET

I shall consider the National Literacy strategy under four headings: the wider social and intellectual context; the NLS document as itself a text; the theoretical underpinnings; and future directions.

NLS in Context

It is important to consider the Government's obsession with falling standards and with raising achievement in literacy in the broader context of public attention to literacy over time. Freebody (see AILA website, 1999), amongst others, has drawn attention to the recurrent public crises over literacy (Street, 1999). Brooks (1997) of NFER has produced the most authoritative survey of literacy levels as measured by standard procedures since the war, and concluded that nothing much has changed, although by broader measures the goal posts themselves have been moved and what counts as literacy currently involves more elaborate and sophisticated skills than previously counted. Against this background we need to ask not only why the Government is so obsessed with standards and crises, but why they are focusing on such narrow conceptions of literacy precisely at the point when developments point in the opposite direction. Gee and others' analysis of the New Work Order (Gee *et.al.*, 1996; Holland *et. al.*, 1998) and Kress's (1997) attention to a New Communicative Order suggest alternative directions in which to look when considering what aspects of language and literacy are appropriate for schooling. At the institutional level, we might also consider the plethora of government agencies devoted to setting, monitoring and evaluating literacy standards – NLF; NC; QCA; Ofsted; BSA – a veritable Foucauldian surveillance.

NLS as Text

Analysing the National Literacy Strategy document as itself a text can reveal underlying conceptions and assumptions that might help us answer the questions raised above. Within the genre of public policy documents more generally, we could address the modality evident both in linguistic items – *should, essential, need* – and in the layout and format – *lists, bullet points.* In terms of content, there is a tendency to privilege aspects of literacy concerned with instruction and control, such as public information and instructional texts, e.g. p. 39, Yr4, Term 2:

- to identify features of non-fiction texts in print and IT, e.g. *headings, lists, bullet points, captions* which support the reader in gaining information efficiently).

It is interesting to note here that the genre being privileged is exactly that of the document itself which uses bullet points that I would argue in this context constitute categorical modality. Questioning of authority, alternative meanings, and attention to other texts and genres, on the other hand, are less in evidence. The division between 'fiction' and 'non-fiction', by allocating interpretation, challenge and analysis of ideology to 'fiction', contributes to the treatment of public documentation as neutral and not subject to such critical scrutiny.

Theory

The National Literacy Strategy is firmly rooted in an autonomous model of literacy (Street, 1984). It assumes decontextualised skills, competencies, basics, a sequence from isolated to more complex and situated units, and it privileges written over oral language. This leads to the NLS failing to draw children's attention to a number of key features of literacy. There is little attention to contexts for literacy, such as community literacy practices, contrasts between home and school as social practice and the relations between home and school with respect to literacy learning and activity. Hannon (1998) has pointed out how much 'family literacy' assumes a one way relationship with schooled literacy penetrating the home at the expense of a more dialogic relation of the kind evidenced by the work of Moll (1992), Heath (1983; 1991) etc. An ideological model, on the other hand, conceptualises literacy as social practice and recognises the often hidden ideological and cultural features of literacy in practice. Recent work on academic literacies drawing upon this perspective, has suggested the value of using sociolinguistic and anthropological perspectives to understand the literacy practices and genres associated with writing in educational contexts (Lea & Street, 1999; Ivanic, 1998). This approach, for instance, might attribute apparent 'problems' with such writing to students' concerns around discourse features of writing, such as cohesion, rather than the traditional grammar and spelling issues on which the NLS focuses. Attention to register and to the effects and functions of linguistic resources and choices as outlined by Halliday and Systemic Linguistics; and to when and how to use resources as suggested by Hymes, Cazden and others in the Ethnography of Communication tradition, could all enhance this rather narrow syllabus.

Future Directions

Questions raised by the attention to context and theory proposed here include:

- how do teachers already developing complex language work and projects (e.g. multilingual projects) adapt these to the Literacy Hour and NLS?
- how might the above 'missed' features of context and text be incorporated into the present framework?
- what would a curriculum look like that included these?

It is odd, as Sealey says here, that the two major sources of knowledge about language in context are scarcely drawn upon for this Programme.

Implied Theories of Language in the National Literacy Strategy

ALISON SEALEY

Whatever we may think about the innovations in teaching represented by the National Literacy Strategy, and however much we may welcome its avowed philosophy of including all pupils in the practice of literacy, as well as its recognition that reading and writing involve engagement with actual texts and a wide range of purposes and audiences, a key concern for applied linguists is the nature of the theory of language which underpins this national strategy. From my reading of the central *Framework* document and the training package of materials for teachers, I would suggest that the NLS is less than fully explicit about how language – and particularly grammar – is to be conceptualised, and that there are internal inconsistencies in what it implies about these matters.

A comparison with the LINC (Language in the National Curriculum, n.d.) materials is illuminating, because these did engage explicitly with theories about language. The LINC materials expressed a commitment to a Hallidayan, functional model of language, recognising that the *macro-level* issues of social and political relations are inseparable from *micro-level* choices manifest in words and sentences. The side-stepping of this issue in the NLS leads to some odd assertions about the nature of language. I have commented on these in greater detail and with specific examples elsewhere (Sealey, 1999), but here I will simply highlight three general problems which I find with these materials.

Firstly, the division of the NLS into *Word level work*, subheaded *phonics, spelling and vocabulary*; *Sentence level work*, subheaded *grammar and punctuation*; and *Text level work*, subheaded *comprehension and composition* makes it difficult to explore the interrelationships between them, despite statements in the Framework that this is what is intended. Hence potentially useful conceptual tools such as *discourse, register* and *semantic field*, for example, which cross the boundaries between word, sentence and purpose, are absent or limited, and there is a real danger that language will be represented in an atomised way.

A second problem is a tension between descriptive and prescriptive approaches to language, which may be due to the influences of the different authors who have contributed to the package, or it may be a product of the different aims (pedagogic and political) which the strategy has to address. Thus matters of style and choice are sometimes represented as matters of *correctness,* and the vexed notion of *appropriateness* (by whose judgement?) is taken as given rather than recognised as problematic.

Thirdly, some of the definitions of linguistic terms provided in the glossary are not consistent with those found in contemporary works of linguistic reference. Pupils and teachers have a right to be able to turn with confidence to the Framework as a source of reference, particularly if their own prior study and training has not given them confidence in their metalinguistic knowledge. In its initial published form, the Framework does not justify such confidence. Applied linguists have grounds for concern that such a high-profile, well-funded, national strategy could initially publish teaching materials which fail to take account of current thinking about basic linguistic issues.

I think the NLS does provide an opportunity for attention to language as an important area of learning and understanding in the classroom. I think applied linguists should be working with practitioners to try to ensure its success. Part of this work involves disseminating the knowledge about language to which academic research has contributed and which is shared within the academic community.

Editor's Postscript

Since this symposium, debate about the National Literacy Strategy has continued – within BAAL, within the Committee for Linguistics in Education (CLIE), and within the Linguistics Association of Great Britain (LAGB). Members of LAGB made representation to those responsible for the Strategy about errors in the Glossary of Terms, and at the time of writing it seems likely that this is to be revised as a consequence. Discussions on the model of grammar used within the *Literacy Framework* have been proposed to the NLS team by BAAL, this dialogue taking place in an attempt to begin to build on and extend the interest in language aroused in schools by these first materials, along some of the lines discussed within these symposium papers.

Appendix

Glossary of acronyms

DfEE — Department of Education and Employment
ITT — Initial Teacher Training
NC — National Curriculum
NLF — National Literacy Framework
OFSTED — Office for Standards in Education
QCA — Qualifications and Curriculum Authority
TTA — Teacher Training Agency

References

Barton, D. and Hamilton, M. (1999) *Local Literacies*. London: Routledge.
Barton, D. (1994) *Literacy: An introduction to the ecology of written language*. Oxford: Blackwell.
Brooks, G. (1997) Trends in standards of literacy in the UK 1948–1996. Paper given to British Educational Research Association.
Freebody, P. (1998) Assessment as Communal Versus Punitive Practice: Six new literacy crises AILA *Virtual Seminar series* www.education.uts.edu.au/AILA/VirtSem
Gee, J. (1991) *Social Linguistics: Ideology in discourses*. London: Falmer Press.
Gee, J., Hull, G. and Lankshear, C. (1996) *The New Work Order: Behind the language of the new capitalism*. London: Allen & Unwin.
Halliday, M. (1985) *An Introduction to Functional Grammar*. London: Edward Arnold.
Hannon, P. (1998) How can we foster children's early literacy development through parental involvement? In S. Neuman and K. Roskos (eds) *Children Achieving: Instructional practices in early literacy* (pp. 121–43). Newark DE: International Reading Association.
Heath, S. B. (1983) *Ways with Words*. Cambridge: Cambridge University Press.
Heath, S. B. and Mangiola, L. (1991) *Children of Promise: Literate activity in linguistically and culturally diverse classrooms*. Washington DC: NEA/American Educational Research Association.
Holland, C., Cooke, T. and Frank, F. (1998) *Literacy and the New Work Order: An international literature review*. London: NIACE.
Ivanic, R. (1997) *Writing and Identity*. Amsterdam: John Benjamins.
Kress, G. (1997) *Before Writing: Rethinking the paths to literacy*. London: Routledge.
Kress, G. and van Leeuwen, T. (1996) *Reading Images: The grammar of visual design*. London: Routledge.
Lea, M. and Street, B. (1998) Student writing and faculty feedback in higher education: An academic literacies approach. *Studies in Higher Education* 23 (2), 157–72.
Lea, M. and Street, B. (1999) Writing as academic literacies: Understanding textual practices in higher education. In C. Candlin and K. Hyland (eds) *Writing: Texts, processes and practices* (pp. 62–81). London: Longman.
LINC (n.d.) *Language in the National Curriculum: Materials for professional development*. Nottingham: University of Nottingham.
Lyotard J.-F. (1984) *The Postmodern Condition: A report on knowledge*. Translated by G. Bennington and B. Massumi. Manchester: Manchester University Press.

Moll, C., Amanti, C., Neff, D. and Gonzales, N. (1992) Funds of knowledge for Teaching: Using a qualitative approach to connect homes and classrooms. *Theory into Practice* XXXI (2), 131–41.

Sealey, A. (1999) *Theories about Language in the National Literacy Strategy*. Coventry: Centre for Elementary and Primary Education, University of Warwick.

Street, B. (1984) *Literacy in Theory and Practice*. Cambridge: Cambridge University Press.

Street, B. (1999) New literacies in theory and practice: What are the implications for language in education? *Linguistics and Education* 10 (1), 1–24.

2 Literacy and Oracy Assessment in an Early Years Intervention Project: The roles of English Language stages

SHEENA GARDNER and PAULINE REA-DICKINS
University of Warwick

Abstract

The research for this article took place in the English national context of proposed changes to EAL assessment policy, and in the inner-city local context of an intervention project where Language Support Teams work with children for whom English is an Additional Language at Key Stage One (ages 5–7). Following an overview of some formative and summative assessment practices within the project, the paper examines the diverse uses made of English Language Stages (or Scales, or Levels, or Steps), and argues that for EAL assessment, they not only provide a general reference point which facilitates communication between stakeholders and illustrates the focus of language development work, but they are also a primary form of cultural capital, embodied in the Language Support Teams, objectified in the Stage descriptors, and institutionalised through the uses described in the paper. To abandon a system of separate assessment for EAL, would be to change the system irrevocably for English Language Support professionals.

Introduction

Issues of literacy and oracy assessment for learners for whom English is an Additional Language (EAL) are not new (e.g. Barrs *et al.*, 1990; Keel 1994;

14

Cline & Frederickson 1996) but it is only relatively recently that these have been formally recognised nationally within the context of the National Curriculum (e.g. Leung & South, 1995; SCAA, 1996a; Gillborn & Gipps, 1996).

The most recent report from the Office for Standards in Education (OFSTED, 1997), based on visits to 51 schools and questionnaires from 92 Local Education Authorities (LEAs), reviews the range, quality and value of assessment procedures in use, and questions whether additional English Language (EL) Scales[1] for bilingual pupils are still needed, given the National Curriculum and its associated assessment procedures. The arguments for abandoning EL Scales follow from the first five main findings of their report:

(1) Nationally there is no consistent approach to assessing the competence of bilingual pupils in English and assuring that resources are targeted equitably. Most LEAs use additional English language stages of some kind. ...

(2) There is a tension between the use of English language stages at LEA level as a monitoring tool for funding purposes and their use in schools for identifying and helping to meet individual pupil needs. While many LEAs continue to use data on stages to provide an overview of need in their schools and to monitor progress at a general level, teachers find the data of limited value at classroom level.

(3) Although Language Support Services commonly believe that data on English Language Stages should help teachers plan their teaching more effectively for bilingual pupils, it is clear that this is rarely the case. The majority of Section 11[2] teachers do not use English language stages data for lesson planning. ...

(4) At classroom level, and especially where S11 support is effective, teachers generally ensure that planning and assessment practices work well for bilingual pupils, even though in the majority of schools visited EAL and mainstream assessment systems are not fully integrated.

(5) A lack of consistency in the structure and use of EL scales and uncertainties about the reliability of the data obtained from them are matters of concern. There is little formal agreement trialling or moderation either at LEA or school level of the stages awarded.

(OFSTED, 1997: 3)

The response of NALDIC (National Association for Language Development in the Curriculum) challenges a number of OFSTED's (1997) conclusions, including the validity of exclusively using assessment levels normed for native speakers with EAL learners. It questions 'why a national arrangement for stages to facilitate the equitable distribution of resources has not been put in place, as the logical conclusion to overcome inconsistencies in LEA practices, [and] why a serious study was not set up to look into EAL assessment, for formative purposes, drawing on research and studies conducted elsewhere, and making recommendations for consultation with professionals' (South, 1997: 4). Reviewing EAL assessment in the USA and Australia, Cameron and Bygate (1997) caution against adopting scales that have not been validated by classroom evidence in a British context.

This paper provides a contribution to the debate on EL Scales by examining the role of one particular set, the City of Coventry *Model Assessment Sheets* (MAS), in literacy and oracy assessment in an Early Years Intervention Project. We first describe the research context from which our data is drawn. We then discuss three related issues that characterise the assessment contexts: collaboration between the class teacher and the language support teacher; expectations and expertise of each in relation to the assessment of literacy and oracy at Key Stage 1; and issues of integration and separation of language and content. Within this context, we explore and critique the use of the Coventry Model Assessment Sheets, as an example of EL Scales.[3] Our concluding discussion compares our findings with those of OFSTED. Although Coventry schools were not visited in the OFSTED survey, the main findings of our study are similar to OFSTED's in many respects, but they differ in our suggesting a central, pivotal role for EL Scales, with their significance as cultural capital, and raise concerns about abandoning autonomous assessment in English Language Support work.

The Early Years Intervention Project Research Context[4]

The research is part of an on-going project in the nine inner city primary schools in Coventry where the Early Years Intervention Project (EYIP) is being implemented to address problems of low levels of achievement in English. Density of learners with EAL was an important selection criterion for inclusion in the EYIP which deploys nine fte (full-time equivalent) Language Support Co-ordinators and 30 fte Bilingual Education Assistants predominantly in Key Stage 1 (KS1) Year One classes.

The overall aim of the EYIP is to ensure that by the end of Year Two all pupils in the nine partner schools will be able to gain access to the National Curriculum (NC), and that the percentage of children in these schools achieving Level 2 or above in KS1 of the NC Teacher Assessments for English will, over the lifetime of the project, move towards the national average.

The research initially centred on assessment procedures and processes from the perspective of different stakeholder groups: Class Teachers (CTs), Language Support Co-ordinators (LSCs) and Bilingual Education Assistants (BEAs). The methodology included a survey to all stakeholders to elicit main assessment issues; a questionnaire to all EYIP LSCs to gather essentially quantitative data; a structured interview in each of the nine schools; and classroom observations.

The results suggest that the EYIP is very effective and that well co-ordinated assessment procedures contribute significantly to this. In this respect our findings endorse recent OFSTED inspection reports on the schools.

Language, Literacy and Oracy: Issues of collaboration, integration and expertise

The assessment practices in the schools – the contexts in which the EL Scales are used – varies greatly. In some schools EYIP project staff work very productively together with class teachers, planning together, jointly assessing at times, with each focusing on their own area of responsibility. So, for example, exploratory functions such as expressing cause and effect were assessed during science units, thus linking the NC science objectives to the relevant communicative functions, along the lines of Mohan *et al.*'s integrative assessment (1996).

In other schools, there were clearly tensions between the expectations of the class teachers and those of the LS Team, and a number of LSCs strongly put forward the view that their responsibility was language acquisition, and not literacy related skills.

- Raising awareness of mainstream teachers as to the type of assessments we carry out, i.e. punctuation, handwriting and spelling do not form part of an assessment of language acquisition ....   (Ph1,08,LSC,3)

A variation of this was found in schools where responsibilities fell more along an oracy vs literacy divide with the LS Team focused on oracy and the class teacher on literacy. This results partly from the emphasis on oracy in the Coventry Model Assessment Sheets, and its relative lack of emphasis in the National Curriculum, particularly when compared with Literacy and Numeracy. The following quotation from an LSC illustrates the contrast.

- She [the CT] assesses them from a NC Performance Level. I've [LSC] got a good working knowledge of it. But I'm not sufficiently and equally as expert. She can hear a child read and can say '2C'. Whereas I can talk to a child and usually, say B+/C-.   (Ph3,C,R1,591-595)

In most schools, however, the LSC was clearly valued for her understanding of the nature of language development in the EAL context and of language itself (an area some primary teachers perceive as a weakness in their own practice [Williamson & Hardman, 1995]). Indeed, it is clear that in the absence of a fully-articulated official approach (syllabus, methodology, materials, etc.) to EAL nationally or in the LEA (SCAA, 1996b notwithstanding), the primary written testimony to the LS Team's expertise is the EL Stages. Despite all the natural and contextual variation in their use, they are central to legitimising the EAL work in schools.

OFSTED's main finding (iv) was that 'at classroom level, and especially where S11 support is effective, teachers generally ensure that planning and assessment practices work well for bilingual pupils, even though in the majority of schools visited EAL and mainstream assessment systems are not fully integrated'. The findings of the present study corroborate both simple propositions but do not support their conjunction with *even though*. From the EYIP perspective, it is appropriate that the assessment systems are not fully integrated, given the different responsibilities and areas of expertise, including insight into EAL language development, of the LSC and CT.

Widespread use does not mean they are flawless. Moreover, many scales were influenced by the EL Stages developed 'out of a particular context, and a particular time' (Hester, 1996: 182). The Coventry Model Assessment Sheets are no exception, and an analysis of their main features suggests ways they could be improved in the light of experience and developments in EAL pedagogy and policy, as well as the changing mainstream context. For example, closer links could be drawn between the descriptors in the scales and the National Curriculum content.

Overall, the support for relating EAL assessment to steps toward the NC was highly qualified (Ph2, Q.24). 'It seems appropriate.' It was felt that it might be possible to build on the NC reading objectives, and possibly writing, but that the oracy objectives were 'disappointingly vague and narrow', and that to limit EAL assessment to English, would miss much important language required for effective communication in other curriculum areas, such as science. It would also lose an important insight into the extent to which children's NC performance might be limited by their English language proficiency, and vice versa:

- [if] context for language utterances ... [are] not given ... assessment may be unreliable. a child struggling with a new concept may not perform at the same level with language as when secure with concepts.

                                                                                                (Ph1,18,LSC,3)

The Use of English Language Scales in the EYIP Context

The assessment framework of the EYIP is presented in Table 1. In addition to the procedures that relate to the EL Scales, there are standardised and statutory assessments, as indicated in Table 1. Among these, the British Picture Vocabulary Test (BPVS) is worthy of comment.

Table 1 Assessment framework

Assessment Procedures	Nature of Procedures	Pupils Assessed	Person(s) Involved	When/How Often	Use
1. EAL Baseline assessment	assessment of L1 and English abilities, includes background & developmental information as well as language	EAL pupils who are new to the EYIP	BEA, LSC, and maybe parents	around entry to school	to gather baseline information to inform teaching and against which to measure progress. Presumably will supplement statutory Baseline Assessment from Sept. 98
2. Language sampling	samples of EAL children's language is gathered from different contexts	EAL	BEAs and LSC	regularly	a. to inform teaching and monitor progress b. to inform the LAA c. selected samples entered on LDR to illustrate progress
3. Linguistic Ability Assessment (LAA)	summative assessment based on Model Assessment Sheet descriptors and language samples, scored Level A-E in oracy, reading, writing and overall	EAL	LSC	twice yearly, autumn and summer	used to monitor language development of targeted EAL pupils for EYIP purposes starts in Reception
4. Language Development Record (LDR)	record from Nursery to Year 6 with background information, EAL support, LAAs, KS1 and KS2 results	EAL	LSC	entries made when acquired	a cumulative profile of the child's ability and achievement to share with/pass to other teachers
5. Linguistic Ability Return (LAR)	record from each school of number of pupils at each Level (A-E) by heritage	EAL	LSC	annually in Jan/Feb.	to inform staffing decisions for September to monitor trends
6. Other teacher assessment	teacher developed or adopted procedures	EAL, EMT or all children	LSC, CT & sometimes both together	regularly	to monitor progress, or other may be noted on LDR
7. School-based assessment	some schools use standard assessments e.g. Salford Reading Test	EMT and sometimes EAL	CT and sometimes LSC	varies	to monitor progress, or other may be noted on LDR
8. NC KS1 End of year assessments	Teacher Assessments and Standard Achievement Tasks administered to all pupils who are entered	EAL and EMT	CT sometimes with BEA	in May of Year 2	a measure of EAL pupils' ability to access the curriculum noted on LDR
9. British Picture Vocabulary Scale (BPVS)	standardised test of all pupils' ability to name objects and events in pictures; strictly controlled 1-1 procedure	EAL and EMT	LSC	twice yearly; November & June	used primarily as a standardised measure to demonstrate gains for funding purposes; external measure to language development and NC teaching

The BPVS, a standardised measure, has been successfully used to demonstrate pupil achievement for funding purposes. For example, in the first seven months of the project, the average age equivalence score increased from 16.6 to 9 months behind chronological age (Coventry City Council, 1997: 7). Results from the statutory KS1 Assessments at the end of Year Two can also be considered significant indicators of the success of the project, and indeed in many schools they have been very rewarding.

The BPVS is a summative measure, and although time-consuming to administer, its value to the project is recognised in that its administration is strictly controlled; it has been normed on L1 and bilingual learners; it responds to progress at beginner level; and it is essentially external to the language development and mainstream curricula.

The tension related to different uses of EL Stages (OFSTED, 1997: 3ii) is reduced by the use of the BPVS for funding purposes. The BPVS takes time away from teaching, its results are of limited value at classroom level, and the need to continually apply for funding is detrimental to long term planning, but its use does supplement that of the EL Stages which are employed in less controlled, non-standardised contexts. The use of the BPVS itself is not ideal, however, and our research suggests that a nationally recognised set of EL Stages with suggested assessment tasks and detailed sample responses would be welcomed, 'if it was a good one' (Ph2, Q.25). Respondents were virtually unanimous in their commitment to some separate assessment for pupils with EAL (in addition to mainstream assessment), particularly to show progress at the lower levels (Ph.2, Q.22).

As South (1977: 4) points out, knowledge of EL Stages provides a general reference point which does not of itself inform lesson planning, and is not designed as a tool for formative assessment. It is precisely this use as a reference point that means it can form a link between different assessment functions and provide teachers with a means of talking about language proficiency not only with each other, but also with others in the school, parents, Section 11 management and outside agencies. In the EYIP, the EL Stages are involved, to varying degrees, in six different assessment-related procedures. The nature and use of each is outlined in Table 1, with comments on variation in practice and issues that arise below.

(1) Use of Coventry Model Assessment Sheets in Baseline Assessment

Although the EYIP Baseline Assessment is wider in scope than the EL Scales, it does include initial assessment of proficiency in both mother tongue (MT) and English. Such assessment typically refers to the EL Scales both in terms of Stages, and in terms of descriptors at a given Stage.

(2) Use of Coventry Model Assessment Sheets in Language Sampling

The assumptions underlying Language Sampling are that reliable assessment requires a cumulative record; and evidence for particular assessments should be observable. The issues raised relate to how representative the samples are, and how accurately spoken samples in particular are recorded.

There was considerable variation in terms of how samples were collected and used, some of which were greatly influenced by the EL Stages, and others much less so. Some samplers had a convergent approach, looking for specific language performance, while others, like the BEA cited below, wrote things down and looked for patterns later.

- I write things down ... thinking 'Oh this is just a couple of words' but then a day later ... he says something and he's always saying that, and I would write it down for you [the LSC] because then I know that he's not progressed. (BEA,E,R4,295–301)

One LSC takes booklets of language samples home each week to select from and clearly used her review of the samples related to the EL Stages to inform the next weeks' teaching. Another LSC gathered samples each term from work completed and notes made during the term. Such variation in the use of the EL Scales in Language Sampling reflects healthy differences in approaches to assessment, but clearly an appropriate set of EL Stages can be of great benefit in language sampling, particularly to new professionals joining the project.

(3) Use of Coventry Model Assessment Sheets in the Linguistic Ability Assessment

The most direct use of the Model Assessment Sheets should be in the Linguistic Ability Assessment where the LSCs assign grades for Oracy, Reading, Writing and an Overall (A–E) grade to each targeted pupil. As linguistic progress is not uniform, teachers adopt a best fit approach, matching pupil performance as well as possible to the level descriptors given. The current emphasis of the descriptors is functional and linguistic, but there are also affective descriptors and those that relate to the context and mainstream curriculum (cf. Leung, 1996a). Teachers vary in the attention they pay to the different kinds of descriptor in their assessment; generally there was a feeling that less emphasis could be given to grammatical development and more emphasis to linguistic performance in curricular contexts. Nevertheless, the EL Scales are meaningful to the teachers, and provide a means of talking about their students, as this LSC illustrates.

- Theoretically when we grade them as a D we wouldn't give them support. E's are when they're speaking with their peers. The A's and B's are my remit. The C's and D's, if we have got the staffing, we cannot do a detailed analysis with C's and D's. It's just not feasible anymore. Years ago we could. We still work with the C's, D's and E's because they need role models. We're desperate for role models.   (D,R1,486–95)

Without the EL Stages it would not be possible to group pupils for learning purposes in this way and to target resources to areas of need. Such information is used not only by the Language Support Team (LSC and BEAs), but also by class teachers to inform curricular groupings. While there are arguments for grouping children according to ability in different subject areas, and for creating mixed ability groups, there is also evidence (e.g. Harley *et al.*, 1990) that without particular attention, appropriate language development may not take place, as well as evidence from this EYIP that targeted language intervention is effective.

(4) Use of Coventry Model Assessment Sheets in the Language Development Record

The Language Development Record provides a cumulative picture of the learner which can be shared among professionals in the school. It includes language samples, results of all linguistic and other assessments together with background information and a record of language support received. The issues here relate to integration (see above) and interpretability of the Model Assessment Sheet levels by the class teacher. As the LS Team works within the mainstream classroom, and the children are integrated for some or all activities, the class teachers acquire through experience an understanding of the range of ability of children at each level.

(5a) Use of Coventry Model Assessment Sheets in Linguistic Ability Return

The results of the Linguistic Ability Assessment are summarised on a Linguistic Ability Return, and used, as in many LEAs, 'to provide an overview of need in their schools and to monitor progress at a general level' (OFSTED, 1997: 3,ii). They also allow Section 11 to monitor the movement of EAL needs through the LEA.

As the LAR informs staffing decisions in the following academic year, this could give rise to issues of moderation between schools. Although concerns about moderation were expressed by the respondents (c.f. OFSTED, 1997: 3v), the focus of their concern was professional integrity rather than unfair staffing decisions. They felt that all LSCs should be working to the same standards.

(5b) Use of Coventry Model Assessment Sheets in Relation to Funding

The results from the Linguistic Ability Return, together with school EYIP progress reports and BPVS results, provide information that can strengthen bids for funding and demonstrate that the school is raising levels of achievement in accordance with Government directives. No issues were raised in connection with this use.

(6) Use of Coventry Model Assessment Sheets in Other Teacher Assessment

Other teacher assessment can provide samples of pupil work that can feed into the Linguistic Ability Assessment. The current EL Scales are less relevant in areas such as assessing learning strategies, which are important for accessing the mainstream curriculum in English, and comprehension of the content of the mainstream curriculum, which might be assessed in mother tongue. Findings from such assessments may be entered on the Language Development Record.

Discussion and Conclusions

As has been shown above, the Coventry Model Assessment Sheets are used formatively to inform teaching, language support and class management, and summatively to make judgements about learner achievement, and decisions in levels of targeting for groups across the schools. They are used in communication with the full range of professional staff as well as parents. In this respect, our findings are very different from those reported by OFSTED (2, 3, 4).

Whilst the present study does support many of the findings in the OFSTED report, it interprets them differently: There are problems with the Stage Level Descriptors, but this is seen as reason to revise them, not discard them. Assessment of EAL and NC is not always integrated, and this is appropriate for language does not develop apace with curricular ability and both are important. Nevertheless it was recognised that 'It is intrinsically important for the EAL assessment frameworks to have a regard to the National Curriculum' (Leung, 1996a: 200). The EL Levels are referred to by many different stakeholders for different purposes that are sometimes at odds, but in this way, they provide a general reference point which facilitates communication between stakeholders and illustrates the focus of language development work.

Ultimately, the OFSTED findings call into question the value of EAL Scales, but our findings suggest an alternative. If we look at the three forms of cultural capital (Bourdieu, in Luke, 1996: 328), EAL assessment is *embodied* in the Language Support Teachers; *objectified* in the EL Scales; and *institutionalised* through the formative and summative uses outlined above. If the EL Scales were to be abandoned, how would the embodied knowledge and skills (cultural capital) of EAL assessment be institutionalised? From an ecological perspective, 'texts cannot be isolated from practices' (Barton, 1994: 64) and indeed the Model Assessment Sheets in Coventry have taken on a significance far beyond the

343e43 444b44444344b3453344r44

words used to describe the Stages. In the absence of EL Scales, what would shape EAL assessment events and practices? What written object could the LSC point to and say 'this is what we do' ('this is who we are')? These uncertainties threaten to devalue EAL assessment itself, for 'ultimately capital is only capital if it is recognised as such' (Luke, 1996: 329).

Acknowledgements

We would like to thank Emma Clayton, Chris Shearsby, Sandra Howard, Hugh South, Teresa O'Brien and the BAAL Advisory Board for helpful comments on previous versions of this paper.

Notes

1. A range of terms is used in the UK, Australia, Canada and the United States to describe these performance descriptors. These include ESL (English as a Second Language) profiles, bandscales, stages, scales, steps, benchmarks and attainment targets. In this paper, we follow OFSTED, who talk of a scale consisting of several stages, and Coventry, whose five-point scale is described in a series of Model Assessment Sheets, one for each stage (A to E) for each year of the National Curriculum.
   Examples and discussion of ESL/EAL scales are available from a number of sources. The reader may wish to refer to Brindley, 1998; Leung, 1996a,b; McKay & Scarino 1991; or Moore 1996, among others.
2. Section 11 of the Local Government Act 1966 provides grants to local authorities, amongst others, to address disadvantage brought about by differences of language or culture experienced by members of any ethnic minority in accessing education and other services.
3. Although there is diversity across LEAs in the nature of scales used, the similarity of our findings to OFSTED's leads us to believe that our interpretation of the findings would be valid in many LEAs beyond Coventry and therefore have national significance.
4. The research partnership between Minority Group Support Services and the University of Warwick is funded by a grant from the SRB/Coventry City Council.

References

Barrs, M., Ellis, S., Hester, H. and Thomas, A. (1990) *Patterns of Learning: The primary language record and the national curriculum.* London: Centre for Language in Primary Education.

Barton, D. (1994) *Literacy: An introduction to the ecology of written language.* Oxford: Blackwell.

Bridley, G. (1998) Outcomes-based assessment and reporting in language learning programmes: A review of issues. *Language Testing* 15 (1), 45–85.

Cameron, L. and Bygate, M. (1997) Key issues in assessing progression in English as an additional language. In C. Leung and C. Cable (eds) *English as an Additional Language: Changing Perspectives.* Watford: NALDIC

City of Coventry (n.d.) Section 11 Language Support Projects Linguistic Ability Survey. Model Assessment Sheets.

Cline, T. and Frederickson, N. (eds) (1996) *Curriculum Related Assessment, Cumins and Bilingual Children.* Clevedon: Multilingual Matters.

Coventry City Council (1997) Coventry City Council SRB Challenge Fund Round 3 Project Development and Appraisal Form. v2.7 13/6/97.

Gillborn, D. and Gipps, C. (1996) *OFSTED Reviews of Research: Recent research on the achievements of ethnic minority pupils.* London: HMSO.

Harley, B., Allen, P., Cummins, J., and Swain, M. (eds) (1990) *The Development of Second Language Proficiency.* Cambridge: Cambridge University Press.

Hester, H. (1996) The stages of English learning: The context. In *Invitational Conference on Teaching and Learning English as an Additional Language.* London: SCAA.

Keel, P. (ed.) (1994) *Assessment in the Multi-Ethnic Primary School.* Stoke-on-Trent: Trentham Books.

Leung, C. and South, H. (1995) The assessment of EAL pupils: A discussion paper for members. Watford: NALDIC.

Leung, C. (1996a) An Investigation of Current Practice in Assessing Stages of Language Acquisition. In *Invitational Conference on Teaching and Learning English as an Additional Language.* London: SCAA.

Leung, C. (1996b) English as an additional language within the national curriculum. *Prospect* 11 (2), 58–68.

Luke, A. (1996) Genres of power? Literacy education and the production of capital. In R. Hasan and G. Williams (eds) *Literacy in Society* (pp. 308–38.). London: Longman.

McKay, P. and Scarino, A. (1991) *The ESL Framework of Stages.* Melbourne: Curriculum Corporation.

Moore, H. (1996) Telling what is real: Competing views in assessing ESL development. *Linguistics and Education* 8 (2), 189–228.

Office for Standards in Education (OFSTED) (1997) *The Assessment of the Language Development of Bilingual Pupils.* London: OFSTED.

School Curriculum and Assessment Authority (SCAA) (1996a) *Invitational Conference on Teaching and Learning English as an Additional Language, London, 27–28 April 1995.* London: SCAA.

School Curriculum and Assessment Authority (SCAA) (1996b) *Teaching English as an Additional Language: A framework for policy.* London: SCAA.

South, H. (1997) OFSTED Report. The Assessment of the Language Development of Bilingual Pupils: A discussion paper for NALDIC.

Williamson, J. and Hardman, F. (1995) Time for refilling the bath? A study of primary student-teachers' grammatical knowledge. *Language and Education* 9 (2), 117–34.

3 The Role of Social Class and Home Literacy Practices in Literacy Proficiency in a Group of Chilean Adolescents

JOHN GIBBONS
University of Sydney
ELIZABETH LASCAR
University of New South Wales
MARÍA ISABEL MIZÓN MORALES
Pontíficia Universidad Católica de Chile

Abstract

This paper discusses the findings of a study conducted in Chile. The study involved 96 Chilean secondary students. It examined the relationship between the frequency of use of various home literacy practices, such as newspaper reading, consultation of encyclopaedias, and the discussion of serious topics demanding complex registers, and the development of the following aspects of literacy as measured by tests: academic register; grammar and vocabulary; basic literacy (spelling and accents). It revealed that there is a significant relationship, and the types of literacy practice that would not normally be regarded of value, such as reading of comic books and magazines, also play a significant role.

Introduction

This paper discusses a project in which we were attempting to discover the extent to which Spanish speaking children develop full control of literate language. We are working with Spanish speaking adolescents in both Chile and Australia, but this paper concentrates on the Chilean group although some Australian data are included for comparison purposes. We use the term 'literacy' in the traditional sense of reading and writing, rather than the extended recent meaning of control of cultural practices in (for instance) 'computer literacy' and 'visual literacy'.

Cummins, in a range of publications Cummins (1977; 1984) has divided the development of language proficiency into two elements, everyday conversational language, and cognitive academic language. The latter he relates to education and literacy, and observes that it is mostly acquired in educational contexts. A cogent attack was mounted on Cummins by Martin-Jones & Romaine (1986), who base their critique partly on the inadequate linguistic modelling of the distinction. In a more recent book, Cummins (1996: 67–8) notes that everyday language is more context embedded, while academic language tends to be context reduced, and, since he is not a linguist, counters the criticism of his linguistic modelling by calling on the work of Biber (1988; 1995) for adequate description and evidence that the distinction has linguistic reality.

Context embeddedness and the reference to Biber's work give two strong indicators of the nature of this phenomenon. Biber describes his work as register analysis, and context embeddedness is a defining feature of the Hallidayan register parameter 'mode', which examines the linguistic effects produced by the distance (in terms of time, space and abstractness) between a text and the context to which it refers, and also the distance between listener/reader and speaker/writer. In the bilingualism literature, this type of register variation is often associated with literacy, for instance Hamers & Blanc (1989: 68) refer to 'the "literacy" use of language which requires a decontextualised use of language'. In referring to this register as literate register, we are not claiming that this register equates with literacy, but there is a strong case that it constitutes an important element of literacy – see for example Baynham (1995) Christie (1990) and Halliday (1996). Halliday (1996: 349) writes 'if we say that someone is literate it means that they are effectively using the lexicogrammatical patterns that are associated with written text'.

Literacy is a complex and multifaceted phenomenon. The study of literacy over the last 20 years has moved from a preoccupation with cognitive aspects of literacy, to the study of micro-social aspects of literacy, i.e. literacy practices and the relation of these to the macro-social, i.e. culture, particularly in relation to ethnicity and social class. This paper attempts to address the linkages between all three aspects of literacy, particularly the register aspect of literacy proficiency, home literacy practices, and social class. Our question then is how do home literacy practices affect the development of literate register, and how are the development of literate register and home literacy practices related to socioeconomic status. Much work on literacy has tended to focus on English: this paper looks instead at Spanish.

Cognitive literacy proficiency includes basic literacy, particularly concepts of print, spelling and punctuation. There are textual phenomena such as the understanding of formatting (for instance recognising in a newspaper which parts are advertisements, headlines, news and editorials). Literacy also involves the deployment of background knowledge, and, it may be argued, the ability to recognise a writer's ideological base. At the interface between social context and proficiency, are register based aspects of literacy, which deploy in a manner unlike everyday language the grammatical and lexical resources of the language.

Literacy practices are socially situated, and commonly involve both speech and writing (Baynham, 1995). We are particularly interested in culturally based literacy practices (see Baynham, 1995; Martin-Jones & Bhatt, 1998; Street, 1993). In survey research such as this it did not prove practical to do justice to the full range of home literacy practices – this will be addressed in the next ethnographic phase of this project. We have therefore limited our survey to the frequency, or more accurately the recency, of key literacy events that are not part of the core educational experience. Examples are the reading of comics and magazines, and the home discussion of topics that extend beyond everyday language, such as science, history and politics. The importance of the latter for the development of literacy is discussed in Baynham (1995: 123–57). The instruments that we used to collect data on this issue are in the Appendix.

The understanding of register that is the basis of this study is discussed in some depth in Gibbons (1999). We will therefore summarise briefly here. Register is a product of the relationship between the linguistic systems, and the contexts of their use. So literate academic register is the type of language that is used in the process of education, differing from the registers used every day for social interaction in home and community. Our understanding of literate registers is based upon Biber's description of written register (1988; 1995), on Chafe (1985), Chafe & Tannen (1987), and particularly the work of Halliday and Martin (Halliday & Martin, 1993; Halliday, 1988, 1996; Martin, 1990, 1991). The latter have found 'Field', 'Mode' and 'Tenor' to be linguistic correlates of literate registers. There are certain particular characteristics of register in Spanish that are a consequence of the different lexical and grammatical resources of Spanish. These are described in Gibbons (1999).

To illustrate briefly, we obtained school text books which are used in Argentina and Uruguay to teach Natural Science and Social Science, in years 2 and 3 in primary schools, and in years 7 and 8 in secondary schools. Early in primary school the language of text books needs to be close to everyday language, since young children would not have mastered academic register. By year 7 or 8 however, they are expected to understand it. We then looked for texts which covered closely related topics in the earlier and later years. In other words, texts were extracted which covered similar content, but were written for different ages, in order to see whether there were substantial differences in the language used. Any such differences would indicate the higher levels of academic register that students are expected to handle in the upper years, and would provide evidence of the way register operates in Spanish. We will illustrate with extracts from two of them, one primary and one secondary text. They are presented in columns, with the primary level text in the left column, and equivalents from the secondary level texts to the right, so that the contrasts in the use of the language resources can be clearly viewed.

Table 1 The language of primary and secondary textbooks

Primary	Secondary
El ciclo del agua *The Water Cycle* Al enfriarse las nubes, *When the clouds cool,* las gotitas de agua se juntan the little drops of water join y forman gotas más grandes. *And form bigger drops* Estas gotas, como pesan más, *These drops, since they weigh more,* caen a la tierra en forma de lluvia, nieve y granizo. *Fall to the ground in the form of rain,* *snow and hail.*	**¿Cómo se forman las nubes?** *How are clouds formed?* Las precipitaciones tienen lugar *Precipitation takes place* cuando aumenta el tamaño de las partículas de agua o hielo *when the size of the particles of water* *or ice increases* y ellas caen por acción de la gravedad. *and they fall by the action of gravity*
1 lluvia nieve y granizo *rain, snow and hail*	Las precipitaciones *Precipitation* tienen lugar cuando *takes place when*
2 más grandes *(lit. more big)* bigger	aumenta el tamaño de *increases the size of*
3 gotitas de agua *little drops of water*	las partículas de agua *particles of water* o hielo y *or ice and*
4 caen a la tierra *they fall to the ground*	ellas caen *they fall*
5 como *since*	por acción de *by the action of*
6 pesan más *they weigh more*	la gravedad *gravity*

These particular extracts describe the same phenomenon, but are written for different age levels – the text on the right is for secondary schools, while the text to the left is for primary schools. Consequently the extract from the secondary text is more academic in register. Gaps in the columns show where there is no direct equivalent in the other text. The differences between these texts and other pairs are analysed in detail in Gibbons (1999).

It seems probable that the type of language on the left is much more likely to be learned through conversation in the home, than the language in the right hand text. Indeed, we argue in Gibbons (1999) and in Gibbons & Lascar (1998) that higher levels of language acquisition appear in part to consist of the development of register, of learning how grammatical resources can be redeployed once they have been mastered. So Halliday (1996: 349) writes of nominalisations (which distinguish examples 2, 5 and 6 above) that they occur later '1. diachronically, in the history of the language; 2. developmentally in the history of the individual; 3. instantially, in the history of the text.' In summary, register features appear to be developmental in nature.

Methodology

As we have already noted, there is a large literature on home literacy practices – for a survey see Baynham (1995). Most research has been ethnographic in nature. However, we wished to examine the interaction of home literacy practices and literacy proficiency, so substantial numbers of subjects were required to permit us to examine such interaction in a rigorous manner. We therefore used a survey method for the literacy practices, and objective tests to measure the development of literate register.

Home literacy practices

On the basis of the literature, and with help from Gordon Wells of the Ontario Institute for Studies in Education, we developed a battery of questions concerning literacy practices. These were developed originally for Australian conditions, where Spanish is a minority language, and in the second generation English is usually the dominant language. When we deployed them in Chile we included some measures inappropriate to the Chilean context for comparison purposes. This paper will focus only on those relevant to the mother tongue context. These questions on home literacy practices are given in the Appendix.

Proficiency measures

Register elements

In Gibbons & Lascar (1998) we discuss the methodology developed to discover the nature of the literate register demanded by education, and the instruments developed to measure control of this literate register. The main instrument developed to measure mastery of academic register is a multiple choice cloze based on the high school science text presented earlier in this paper. This test was used only after testing of its reliability (see Gibbons & Lascar, 1998). .

Other elements of literacy

A measure of linguistic aspects of literacy was included in this investigation. It was a C-Test (Klein-Braley & Raatz, 1984; Alderson, Clapham & Wall, 1995: 56), which measures control of vocabulary and morphology – a salient feature of Spanish, and one that is not always fully mastered – see Silva-Corvalán (1991). We also looked at the subjects' responses to see whether they made errors in spelling and punctuation (including accents). Although Spanish spelling is more phonemic than English, one subject's error 'habeses' for 'a veces', shows errors in word division, 'b' for 'v', 'h' for 'ø', and 's' for 'c'. In these cases, and in some others, the same South American Spanish speech sound (or lack of one) has more than one written form. The number of such errors was obtained for each subject, and then subjected to a formula to control for missing words. We refer to this area as 'basic' literacy.

Self assessment of literacy proficiency

Following Hamers (1994), we included measures by which the students assessed their own feelings concerning the ease or difficulty of various literacy acts such as reading a newspaper. While this might not be considered an objective measure, such measures have often correlated well with objective measures, and more importantly they give a good indication of the subject's **confidence** concerning his/her literacy proficiency.

Socio-economic status

We are using this term (hereafter usually summarised as SES) to signify the demographic measure of social class, rather than the cultural characteristics of social class. This was measured by questions concerning the occupation and level of education of both parents. The education measure was a scale running from primary to postgraduate education. Responses on the occupation item were categorised into: unskilled manual; skilled manual; white collar and small business; and managerial and professional.

Pilot study

The measures described above were piloted on 26 Spanish background students at the University of Western Sydney, and measures which failed to discriminate were eliminated.

The sample

The sample was 100 girls aged around 13 years, from two schools in Santiago de Chile, one a prestigious private school, and one a systemic school. The children from the private school were mainly from upper middle class homes, while those from the systemic school were mainly from lower middle class homes, with a proportion of girls from working class homes. Four of the sample were lost because they did not complete the instruments, leaving a total of 96. We also include some comparison data from 32 Spanish speaking adolescents in Sydney, of varied class backgrounds.

Findings

Individual home literacy practices

Results

Table 2 Frequency of individual literacy practices

Literacy Practice (frequency of use	Chilean Mean	Chilean Std Dev.	Chilean Variance	Australian Mean	Australian Std Dev.	Australian Variance
Encyclopaedia	3.38	1.16	1.35	3.36	0.95	0.90
Dictionary	3.77	1.22	1.48	3.23	1.18	1.38
Religious text	2.87	1.42	2.01	3.65	1.20	1.44
Newspaper	4.25	1.12	1.26	3.29	1.40	1.95
Magazine	3.91	1.05	1.10	3.16	1.32	1.74
Comics	3.26	1.33	1.77	4.03	0.88	0.77
Literature	2.68	1.37	1.76	3.77	1.02	1.05
Library	2.27	1.05	1.11	3.36	0.99	0.97
Politics talk	2.89	1.58	2.48	4.36	0.95	0.90
Science talk	3.27	1.37	1.88	3.61	1.17	1.38
History talk	3.47	1.21	1.45	3.58	1.18	1.39

Chile N = 96; Australian N = 32

The possible score for individual literacy practices ranged from 1 (almost never) to 5 (in the last 24 hours). The most frequent literacy practices of the Chilean sample are newspaper reading and magazine reading. The use of dictionaries and encyclopaedias is also quite frequent. Library use is quite infrequent, mostly in the almost never to once a month area. Among the three topics for home discussion, politics is discussed least frequently, history most frequently and science falls in between.

Discussion

Many of the subjects appear to read a newspaper every day, and this is the most common practice examined here. The differences in the three topics for home discussion are intriguing. The large variance in the politics score would suggest that in the minority of homes where politics is discussed, it is discussed a lot. The pattern for religion is similar, suggesting that among students from religious homes, religious texts are commonly read, whilst in other homes they are not – an unsurprising finding that indicates that these measures are working as expected. These findings contrast with the early results (N = 32) from our Australian study, where politics is the most common of the three topics followed by science and then history – the reverse ordering. The other main contrast with the Australian data is that the use of comics, literature and libraries seems considerably more frequent in Australia.

Individual literacy practices and proficiency

A primary concern of this research was to establish a link between proficiency in literacy and the factors which might influence the development of such literacy.

Results

Table 3 Pearson correlations between individual literacy practices and proficiency test scores

	Scientific Register Test	*C-Test*	*Self Evaluation*
Encyclopaedia	0.17 P = *0.051*	0.27 P = **0.003**	0.28 P = **0.003**
Dictionary	0.09 P = 0.19	0.19 P = **0.03**	0.05 P = 0.32
Religious text	0.11 P = 0.15	0.15 P = 0.07	0.23 P = **0.013**
Newspaper	0.12 P = 0.13	0.04 P = 0.34	0.06 P = 0.27
Magazine	0.13 P = 0.10	0.07 P = 0.26	0.3 P = **0.002**
Comics	0.27 P = **0.004**	0.15 P = 0.08	0.04 P = 0.36
Literature	0.24 P = **0.01**	0.17 P = **0.049**	0.35 P = **<0.001**
Library	0.18 P = **0.042**	0.16 P = *0.059*	0.03 P = 0.4
Politics talk	0.01 P = 0.46	0.11 P = 0.14	0.16 P = *0.058*
Science talk	−0.02 P = 0.42	0.00 P = 0.49	0.21 P = **0.022**
History talk	0.18 P = **0.037**	0.17 P = **0.049**	0.22 P = **0.016**

N = 95 (one missing value);
Correlations better than .05 are in **bold**, borderline cases in *italics*

Discussion

We were pleasantly surprised to find that the role of individual and home literacy practices in the development of literacy, which we would assume would be overwhelmed by school education, proved in a several cases to be significantly related to our proficiency measures. The use of encylopaedias is related to scores on the tests, and unexpectedly fiction (including comics and literature) correlated with the development of scientific register. The findings from the talk categories are unsurprising. Since talk about politics and even science is fairly infrequent, it does not relate to the development of literacy. However, history talk, being more common, is related to the development of literacy as measured by three test instruments. Basic literacy (spelling and punctuation) would appear to be related to reading in general. Note that science talk is marginally correlated with more basic literacy errors.

Groupings of literacy practices

The findings above suggest that groupings of literacy practices such as fiction versus non-fiction might exist. This notion was bolstered by a factor analysis. The groupings were (1) **reading** – only those items related to reading (2) **talk** – i.e. the remaining items which ask about discussion in the home of politics, science and history; the reading items were then sub-grouped into (3) **non-fiction** – the reading items on use of dictionaries, encyclopaedias, newspapers and libraries; and (4) **fiction** – magazines, literature and comics.

Results

Correlations between groups of home literacy practices and the proficiency measures are displayed in Table 4.

Table 4 Pearson correlations between groups of literacy practices and proficiency tests

	Scientific Register Test	*C-Test*	*Self Evaluation*
All literacy practices	0.27 **P = 0.004**	0.28 **P = 0.003**	0.37 **P = <0.001**
Talk	0.07 P = 0.26	0.12 P = 0.12	0.26 **P = 0.006**
Reading	0.34 **P = <0.001**	0.31 **P = 0.001**	0.34 **P = <0.001**
Non-fiction	0.24 **P = 0.009**	0.3 **P = 0.002**	0.19 **P = 0.035**
Fiction	0.32 **P = <0.001**	0.19 **P = 0.03**	0.33 **P = <0.001**

N = 95 (one missing value); Correlations better than 0.05 are in **bold**

Stepwise multiple regression analysis was also performed using the various forms of literacy practices – fiction, non-fiction, and literate talk. When the dependent variables were the science cloze and the C-test both fiction and non-fiction played a role (explaining around 10% of the variance, and being significantly related). However, when the dependent variable was the number of basic literacy errors, it was fiction alone that contributed to the lower rate of basic literacy errors.

Discussion

Overall the more students engaged in the various home literacy practices, the higher were their scores on our literacy measures, as is shown in the first row of Table 4. The relationships revealed here show that the development of register aspects of literacy, grammar and vocabulary and self evaluation of proficiency are all related to active home literacy practices. Furthermore, unlike our Australian sample, when the talk measures (which do not contribute to the scores) are removed, and we look only at reading, this effect is strengthened. We will discuss this finding in the conclusions. It should be noted that correlations such as these do not reveal direction or causation – in other words it is not clear whether greater literacy skills are a result of more reading in the home, or whether reading in the home is a consequence of greater reading skills. It should be noted however, that scientific register contributes to an advanced form of literacy, and it is unlikely that this is acquired **before** the home reading habit, although wide reading could contribute to the development of scientific register, suggesting that any causal flow may be from home literacy practices to better literacy.

The reading of both non-fiction and fiction appear to be related to the development of non-basic aspects of literacy. Basic literacy – spelling and accents – appear to be related to light fictional reading, but not serious non-fiction reading. Another interpretation is that reading for pleasure can play a role in the development of spelling and punctuation. The grouping of talk variables appears to be unrelated to literacy, although it should be noted that this is not true for the most frequent type of talk – history talk – as we noted earlier. The likely explanation for this finding is the comparative infrequency of political and scientific talk.

The role of socio-economic status

The SES measure examined the occupation and level of education of both father and mother. However the mother's occupation did not relate well to the other measures, in all probability because it is common for upper middle class Chilean women not to join the workforce. Therefore the combined measure of SES will use only the data from the mother's educational level, the father's educational level, and the father's occupation. There was some relationship between the SES measures and the test scores, as is shown in Table 5.

Results

Table 5 Correlations: SES measures by tests

	Scientific Register Test	C-Test	Self Evaluation
Father's occupation	0.16 P = 0.055	0.07 P = 0.238	0.18 **P = 0.041**
Father's education	0.17 **P = 0.049**	0.11 P = 0.134	0.2 **P = 0.032**
Mother's education	0.19 **P = 0.031**	0.1 P = 0.158	0.03 P = 0.389
Combined SES measure	0.21 **P = 0.018**	0.12 P = 0.121	0.16 P = 0.057

N = 96; Correlations better than 0.05 are in **bold**

There was no significant relationship between the SES measures and the C-test scores. There are some relations between SES and the Self Evaluation and Register measures. The data reveal a relationship between the mother's educational level and the register score. The table also shows that the confidence of these girls in their own literacy (Self Evaluation) is related to the father's education and employment, but not to the mother's education.

To explore further the relation between SES and Self Evaluation, groups on both measures were established, consisting of approximately the top 25%, the middle 50%, and the bottom 25% (actual sizes of groups were affected by tied scores). The result is given in Table 6.

Table 6 SES groupings crosstabulated by self evaluation groupings

		SES		
Self evaluation				
	Lower	Middle	Higher	Total
Lower	10	10	7	27 (28%)
Middle	13	15	11	39 (40%)
Upper	2*	20	8	30 (31%)
Total	25	45	26	96
	(26%)	(47%)	(27%)	(100%)

Chi-Square 10.061; D.F. 4; Sig. 0.039 (Note one cell less than 5)

The self evaluation measure shows a considerable under-representation of the lower group in the highest self evaluation category (this figure is starred). To see whether this self evaluation was justified, the same groupings were examined for their performance on the science cloze.

Table 7 SES groupings crosstabulated by science cloze groupings

Science Cloze		SES		
	Lower	Middle	Higher	Total
Lower	8	6	5	19 (20%)
Middle	10	26	11	47 (49%)
Upper	7	13	10	30 (31%)
Total	25	45	26	96
	(26%)	(47%)	(27%)	(100%)

Chi-Square 4.792; D.F. 4; Sig. 0.309; Gamma 0.166; Zscore 0.7447

Discussion

The lack of a relationship between SES measures and the C-test shown in Table 5 confirms the widely held view that control of basic grammatical resources does not vary between SES groups. The relationship between the mother's educational level and the development of register may possibly be because mothers tend to be primary care-givers.

Turning to self evaluation, and remembering that the self evaluation measure is in part a measure of **confidence** in one's language abilities, the group from the lower SES rating is under-rating its own abilities – compare the same group's actual scores on the cloze proficiency measure in Table 7, where 7 rather than 2 are in the higher scoring group.

It is clear that there are differences between the class groups on the extent of use of home literacy practices, while at the same time it is important to note that there are subjects from the group rated lower on the SES measure who are in the high group for literacy practices, and vice versa for some subjects from the group rated higher on the SES measure. One possibility is that there is no direct relationship between SES and literacy proficiency, despite the weak relationship revealed in Table 5, but rather that the higher proficiency scores are mediated by literacy practices, which reveal a much stronger relationship with the proficiency measures (see Table 4). In other words, if there is a tendency for students rated higher on the class measure to also have a higher ranking on the use of literacy practices, this may provide the link between class and proficiency.

To test this proposition, the science cloze measure was entered into a stepwise multiple regression analysis as a dependent variable, and the class variable and both the full range of proficiency measures and the reading element of these were included as independent variables. Neither the SES variable nor the full range of literacy measures were entered by the program, as they produced no significant gain over the reading practices measure alone. This seems to show that when the effect of home reading is taken into account, SES played no significant role in scores on the science cloze. Furthermore, when SES was forced into this analysis, it did not contribute to the prediction. In summary, it seems likely that the marginal relationship between SES and literacy is mediated by home literacy practices, and it is these which have a direct relationship with literacy development.

Conclusions

Despite the strong influence exerted upon the development of literacy exercised by formal education, this study provides evidence that home literacy practices may also play a significant role. Also interesting is the fact that it is not only serious reading that plays this role, but also light reading such as magazines and comics, despite the disapproval commonly meted out to such activities. The overwhelming message to emerge here is that in a world where computers, television, radio, video and film can provide much of the entertainment previously derived from reading, regular home reading played a role in the development of literacy in this group of subjects. This finding re-asserts the value of home reading found in many studies, including the Bristol study (Wells, 1981; 1985).

Some intriguing differences emerged between the Chilean and Australian samples. One is for instance tempted to speculate that Chileans became accustomed to avoiding discussion of politics during a period in their recent history when such discussion involved some risk. The higher use of libraries by the Australians may reflect Sydney's high quality system of municipal libraries.

The SES factor was interesting in that it showed that deficit understandings of the relationship between social class and literacy are probably misguided. Home literacy practices were much more significantly related to literacy, and supportive literacy practices were found in some lower SES homes, while poor literacy practices were found in some upper middle SES homes. This also sounds a note of hope, since there is little possibility of changing a school student's SES, but literacy practices do not appear to be rigidly class determined, and are probably more amenable to change. It was disturbing to note the unjustified lack of confidence in their own literacy from the lower social group, indicating that they may have internalised deficit stereotypes of themselves.

Overall the study showed that there are probably linkages between SES and literacy practices, and between literacy practices and literacy proficiency, but it threw into doubt any direct linkage between SES and literacy. Another way of conceiving the issue is not to see social class (as we do here by default) as solely a Weberian concept, based on education and employment, but rather to view class as a broader cultural phenomenon, including forms of behaviour such as literacy practices as suggested by Bourdieu & Passeron (1990). However, this study provides grounds for challenging the view of some writers that SES fully determines cultural practices, particularly literacy practices. Some problems of children from lower SES backgrounds may be rooted in stereotypes and attitudes, rather than substantive differences in behaviour.

Appendix

Note: The approximate translations in brackets were not in the original study.

Estas preguntas se relacionan con lo que tú lees y escribes fuera de las actividades escolares.
(These questions are concerned with what you read and write apart from school work.)

¿Qué tipo de lecturas escoges en un tiempo libre?
(What kind of reading do you do in your spare time?)

¿Qué es lo que más escribes, aparte de las tareas del colegio?
(What do you mostly write, apart from school work?)

Escoje el casillero que mejor refleje tu respuesta.
Las próximas preguntas se relacionan con lo que lees.
(Pick the box which comes nearest to your response.
The following questions are about what you read.)

¿Cuándo fue la última vez que consultaste una **enciclopedia**?
(When did you last use an **encyclopaedia**?)

en las últimas **24 horas** (in the last **24 hours)**	en la última **semana** (in the last **week)**	en el último **mes** (in the last **month)**	en el último **año** (in the last **year)**	**casi nunca** **(almost never)**
☐	☐	☐	☐	☐

¿Cuándo fue la última vez que consultaste un **diccionario**?
(When did you last use a **dictionary**?)

en las últimas **24 horas**	en la última **semana**	en el último **mes**	en el último **año**	**casi nunca**
☐	☐	☐	☐	☐

¿Cuándo fue la última vez que leíste la **Biblia** u otro **texto religioso**?
(When did you last read a **Bible** or other **religious text**?)

en las últimas **24 horas**	en la última **semana**	en el último **mes**	en el último **año**	**casi nunca**
☐	☐	☐	☐	☐

¿Cuándo fue la última vez que leíste un **periódico**?
(When did you last read a **newspaper**?)

en las últimas **24 horas**	en la última **semana**	en el último **mes**	en el último **año**	**casi nunca**
☐	☐	☐	☐	☐

¿Cuándo fue la última vez que leíste una **revista** (ej. Hoy, Qué Pasa, Don Balón, Caras, Cosas, Muy Interesante)?
(When did you last read a **magazine**, eg. … ?)

en las últimas **24 horas**	en la última **semana**	en el último **mes**	en el último **año**	**casi nunca**
☐	☐	☐	☐	☐

¿Cuándo fue la última vez que leíste una **revista de historietas** (ej. Cómic, Condorito, Mafalda, Asterix)?
(When did you last read a **comic book**, eg. … ?)

en las últimas **24 horas**	en la última **semana**	en el último **mes**	en el último **año**	**casi nunca**
☐	☐	☐	☐	☐

¿Cuándo fue la última vez que leíste **por placer** una **obra literaria** (incluyendo ensayo, leyenda, novelas y cuentos)?
(When did you last read **literature for pleasure**, including essays, novels and stories?)

en las últimas **24 horas**	en la última **semana**	en el último **mes**	en el último **año**	**casi nunca**
☐	☐	☐	☐	☐

¿Cuándo fue la última vez que fuiste a una **biblioteca pública** de tu comuna?
(When did you last visit a **municipal library**?)

en las últimas **24 horas**	en la última **semana**	en el último **mes**	en el último **año**	**casi nunca**
☐	☐	☐	☐	☐

Estas preguntas se relacionan con el **habla**.
(These questions are concerned with **speaking**.)

¿Cuándo fue la última vez que hablaste de **política** en casa?
(When did you last discuss **politics** at home?)

en las últimas 24 horas	en la última semana	en el último mes	en el último año	casi nunca
☐	☐	☐	☐	☐

¿Cuándo fue la última vez que hablaste de un tema **científico** en casa?
(When did you last discuss **science** at home?)

en las últimas 24 horas	en la última semana	en el último mes	en el último año	casi nunca
☐	☐	☐	☐	☐

¿Cuándo fue la última vez que hablaste de algún tema **histórico** en casa?
(When did you last discuss **history** at home?)

en las últimas 24 horas	en la última semana	en el último mes	en el último año	casi nunca
☐	☐	☐	☐	☐

References

Alderson, J. C. , Clapham, C. and Wall, D. (1995) *Language Test Construction and Evaluation*. Cambridge: Cambridge University Press.

Baynham, M. (1995) *Literacy Practices: Investigating literacy in social contexts*. London: Longman.

Biber, D. (1988) *Variation Across Speech and Writing*. Cambridge: Cambridge University Press.

Biber, D. (1995) *Dimensions of Register Variation: A cross-linguistic comparison*. Cambridge: Cambridge University Press.

Bourdieu, P. and Passeron, J. C. (1990) *Reproduction in Education, Society and Culture*. (R. Nice, Trans.). London: Sage.

Chafe, W. (1985) Linguistic differences produced by differences between speaking and writing. In D. L. Olson, W. Torrance and Hildgard, A. (eds) *Literacy, Language and Learning* (pp. 105–23). Cambridge: Cambridge University Press.

Chafe, W. and Tannen, D. (1987) The relation between written and spoken language. *Annual Review of Anthropology* 16, 383–409.

Christie, F. (1990) The changing face of literacy. In F. Christie (ed.) *Literacy for a Changing World* (pp. 1–25). Hawthorn, Vic.: Australian Council for Educational Research.

Cummins, J. (1977) Cognitive factors associated with the attainment of intermediate levels of bilingual skills. *Modern Language Journal* 61, 3–12.

Cummins, J. (1984) Wanted: A theoretical framework for relating language proficiency to academic achievement among bilingual students. In C. Rivera (ed.) *Language Proficiency and Academic Achievement*. Clevedon: Multilingual Matters.

Cummins, J. (1996) *Negotiating Identities: Education for empowerment in a diverse society*. Ontario, CA: California Association for Bilingual Education (distributed in UK by Trentham Books).

Gibbons, J. (1999) Register aspects of literacy in Spanish. *Written Language and Literacy* 2 (1), 63–88.

Gibbons, J. and Lascar. E. (1998) Operationalising academic language proficiency in bilingualism research. *Journal of Multilingual and Multicultural Development* 19 (1), 40–50.

Halliday, M. A. K. (1988) On the language of physical science. In M. Ghadessy (ed.) *Registers of Written English: Situational factors and linguistic features* (pp. 162–78). London: Pintner.

Halliday, M. A. K. (1989) Some grammatical problems in scientific English. *Australian Review of Applied Linguistics Series S* (6), 13–37.

Halliday, M. A. K. (1996) Literacy and linguistics: A functional perspective. In R. Hasan and G. Williams (eds) *Literacy in Society* (pp. 339–76). London: Longman.

Halliday, M. A. K. and Martin, J. R. (1993) *Writing Science: Literacy and discursive power*. London: Falmer.

Hamers, J. (1994) How do social networks, attitudes and literacy interact in bilingual development? Paper presented at the Fifth International Conference on Language and Social Psychology, Brisbane.

Hamers, J. and Blanc, M. (1989) *Bilinguality and Bilingualism*. Cambridge: Cambridge University Press.

Klein-Braley, C. and Raatz, U. (1984) A survey of research on the c-test. *Language Testing* 1, 134–46.

Martin, J. R. (1990) Literacy in science: Learning to handle text as technology. In F. Christie (ed.) *Literacy for a Changing World* (pp. 79–117). Hawthorn, Vic.: Australian Council for Educational Research.

Martin, J. R. (1991) Nominalisation in science and humanities: Distilling knowledge and scaffolding text. In E. Ventola (ed.) *Functional Systemic Linguistics: Approaches and uses* (pp. 307–37). Berlin: Mouton de Gruyter.

Martin-Jones, M. and Bhatt, A. (1998) Literacies in the lives of young Gujarati speakers in Leicester. In A. Durgunoglu and L. Verhoeven (eds) *Acquisition of Literacy in Two Languages*. Mahwah, NJ: Erlbaum.

Martin-Jones, M. and Romaine, S. (1986) Semilingualism: A half-baked theory of communicative competence. *Applied Linguistics* 7 (1), 26–38.

Silva-Corvalán, C. (1991) Spanish language attrition in a contact situation with English. In H. Seliger and R. Vargo (eds) *First Language Attrition* (pp. 151–71). Cambridge: Cambridge University Press.

Street, B. (1993) Introduction: The new literacy studies. In B. Street (ed.) *Cross-Cultural Approaches to Literacy* (pp. 1–21). Cambridge: Cambridge University Press.

Wells, G. (1981) *Learning Through Interaction: The study of language development*. Cambridge: Cambridge University Press.

Wells, G. C. (ed.) (1985) *Language, Learning and Education: Selected papers from the Bristol Study, language at home and at school*. Windsor, Berks: NFER Nelson.

4 'How Many Bumps Does a Dromedary Have?': Literacies in the EFL classroom

PAULA KALAJA and ANNE PITKÄNEN-HUHTA
University of Jyväskylä

Abstract

In the past few years, a number of studies have been conducted on reading and writing, or literacy, in L1 school settings. In this study, we have made an attempt to extend the social view of reading and writing to L2 classrooms. More specifically, we looked at one literacy event that took place during an EFL class with year 7 pupils of a secondary school. The event revolved around a text in an EFL textbook. The text engaged the teacher and the pupils in talk (and action). From these it was possible to make inferences about literacy practices in the classroom. We found two competing constructions of literacy to emerge from the data: teacher-imposed literacy and student-imposed literacy, with reading and writing taking on very different meanings in each case. These constructions were constantly negotiated and renegotiated by the participants. Our findings point to the multiple and variable nature of literacy even within one and the same event in the L2 classroom.

Introduction

This article reports on a study which is part of a research project focusing on the teaching and learning of EFL within the Finnish school system (for details, see www.jyu.fi/tdk/hum/englanti/). More specifically, the study is concerned with literacy in an English-as-a-Foreign-Language (EFL) context.

43

One starting point of our study is a social view of reading and writing, or literacies. This means, first of all, that reading and writing are not considered to be separate universal skills generalisable over contexts. Instead, reading and writing are viewed as situated literacy practices which vary from one social group to another and from one context to another, and are, therefore, multiple (Street, 1984, 1995; Barton, 1994; Barton & Hamilton, 1998; Baynham, 1995). Secondly, literacy practices are embedded in broader social practices of particular social groups, like those of a school, for example (Gee, 1996). Finally, the multiple literacies cannot be studied only as internal processes of an individual reader or writer. In other words, we have to go beyond reader/writer-text interaction to the interaction and activities which take place around a piece of written text and which involve a certain group of people (Heath, 1983). From these literacy events it is possible to draw inferences to understand the practices prevalent in particular social settings (Barton & Hamilton, 1998).

Another starting point for this study are a number of interdisciplinary studies on L1 literacy in educational settings (for a review, see Bloome & Green, 1992). Most of these studies have been based either on sociolinguistics (e.g. Bloome, 1993, 1994; Baker & Freebody, 1989) or on Vygotskian views of learning (e.g. Wells, 1990; Maybin & Moss, 1993; Gregory, 1994). Both of these approaches have also been influenced by anthropology and ethnography, and the emphasis has been on interaction in the construction and development of literacy. Consequently, despite the importance of materials, what counts as literacy in the classroom gets its meaning through the practices of working with texts. In the following, the findings of the most relevant of these studies are discussed in greater detail.

Bloome (1989, 1993, 1994) explored reading as a social process in the classroom. His approach was microethnographic, having its basis in sociolinguistic ethnography. He concluded that the interaction between teacher, students and text can be characterised as *text reproduction, procedural display* (including *being a good student*), *cataloguing* and taking a *passive stance* towards the text. *Text reproduction* consists of reading aloud bits of texts or copying exercises; *procedural display* involves the teacher and students displaying successful accomplishment of the lesson; in *cataloguing,* dealing with texts is reduced to listing items found in a text, such as unknown words. This frame was constructed partly on the basis of observed teacher–student interaction and partly on the basis of tasks presented to the students.

In contrast, Wells (1990) takes a Vygotskian perspective on literacy both in and out of educational settings emphasising the importance of talk in making sense of literacy. Wells distinguishes five different modes of engaging with texts in contemporary Western society. These modes are the *performative, functional, informational, re-creational* and *epistemic* modes. They appear to form a hierarchy with the first three being more instrumental and the last two intellectually more demanding. To be fully literate, Wells argues, one should be able to engage with texts epistemically depending on the demands of the situation. His analysis revealed that lack of collaboration in the classroom interactions led to a very superficial engagement with texts. However, a more epistemic mode could be achieved by the teacher actively involving the pupils in scaffolded dialogue.

In their studies, Maybin & Moss (1993) and Moss (1998) have also been influenced by Vygotskian views. They have examined talk related to texts both in and out of classrooms. In describing talk in connection to literacy, they define *talk about text* broadly to include both talk that is closely connected to the reading at hand and talk that refers back to previous readings. They found that classroom readings were collaborative rather than individual and that there were two ways of relating to the text. Firstly, the teacher encouraged the pupils to consider the text as an authority to which they should relate their own experiences. In contrast, the pupils wanted to display themselves as good pupils by extracting interesting details from the text. It was concluded that 'readings are shaped and regulated by the social circumstances in which texts are shared' (p. 146).

In spite of their new insights into L1 literacy in educational settings, the studies reviewed above have some limitations. First, having analysed only parts of literacy events (e.g. a 5-minute segment) around a piece of text rather than entire ones, the studies have not been able to give due recognition to the importance of interaction in the construction of literacies. Secondly, focusing often on the teacher and his/her utterances (e.g. questions) in the classroom, the scholars have not given full acknowledgement to the idea of literacies being jointly constructed by all those involved. Furthermore, these studies have paid little attention to the asymmetry of power relations between the teacher and pupils and its effect on the construction(s) of literacies in the classroom. In other words, literacies are negotiated and renegotiated by the participants in the course of classroom activities, being at times complied with and at other times challenged.

Our study differs from the studies discussed above in that its focus is on L2 literacy. What our study shares with these is a social view of reading and writing, or literacies. Accordingly, we make an attempt to analyse an entire literacy event, from which it is then possible to make inferences about the literacy practices in the classroom. Secondly, we do not expect there to be a single construction of literacy in the EFL classroom; but multiple ones, competing with each other and involving not only the teacher but also pupils. Moreover, the constructions of these literacies are accomplished through talk and action, and, therefore, in our analysis, we also draw on a discourse analytic approach to classroom interaction (e.g. van Lier, 1996; Hancock, 1997).

In what follows, we shall basically be arguing that two constructions of literacy emerge and compete with one another within a specific activity during an EFL lesson involving year 7 secondary school pupils.

Data

Our data consist of observations, and audio- and video-recordings of six consecutive EFL lessons held in a Finnish secondary school. These have been transcribed (for details, see Appendix 1). In addition, we have at hand copies of all teaching materials used by the teacher. The year 7 pupils are 12 or 13 years of age. There are four boys and three girls in the class. English is the second foreign language that the pupils have chosen to study at school (German being the first), and at the time of data collection they had been learning it for over two years.

As we assume literacies to be embedded in broader social practices of a particular group in a particular setting, our analysis of literacies starts from the activities in the classroom. For the purposes of this study, we looked at one specific activity during one of the six EFL lessons. The activity took place around a piece of written text entitled 'Animal Quiz' (see Appendix 2), from an EFL textbook used in the class (Westlake *et al.*, 1995). The pupils were first asked to answer 10 questions concerning various species of animals, then listen to a quiz recorded on tape, with four imaginary characters competing against each other, and after that check if their answers were correct. Importantly, the authors of the textbook had defined this as an exercise in listening comprehension.

The activity starts with the teacher telling the pupils in English, *okay, now we need your notebooks and your textbooks this time, because we are going to listen to an animal quiz.* However, it takes some negotiation and rephrasing of the task before the pupils are ready to go along with the teacher and concentrate on the exercise. It also takes quite a while for them all to have their textbooks, notebooks and pens ready. After answering the questions, listening to the quiz, and checking the correctness of the answers, the activity (with its three stages) is over once the teacher announces to the class that they should move on to another exercise in the textbook, *okay. then we're going to go to menu num- exercise number twenty (0) seven.*

Below are two transcribed excerpts from the first stage of the activity. In these, the pupils are busy answering some of the 10 questions. Translations (in **bold** face) have been provided for those sections where the pupils or the teacher switch codes from English into Finnish, their first language.

In Excerpt 1, the teacher is working on Questions 2 *(How many wings does a horsefly have?)*, 3 *(How deep can a sperm whale dive?)*, and 4 *(How many insects are there in the world today?)* together with the pupils (P stands for an unidentified pupil, F for female, M for male voice):

Excerpt 1

763. **Teacher:** [number two, (0) how many wings] does a horsefly have

764. **Keijo:**   [how many wings does   ]

765. **Teacher:** and you can see that horsefly (0) **is** päa- is päarma,

766. **Teacher:** in Finnish. [so you just (0) guess]=

767. **Teijo:**   [**oh a horsefly**   ]

768. **Keijo:**   [two]

769. **Reijo:**   =no four.

770. **Keijo:**   four.

771. **Teacher:** put (0) put your own [an- guess:] [(0) in the notebook]

772. **Teijo:**   [four <u>wings</u>]

773. **Reijo:**   [**no we won't**   ]

774. **Irja:**   [so]

775. **Irja:**   **what's this ques[tion   ]**

776. **Keijo:**   [how many]

777. **Keijo:**   [bones does the *giraffe* have in] [its neck seven.]

777. **Teacher:** [**how** (0) **many**:   ] [(1)   ]

778. **Keijo:**   [**that one I know too.**]

779. **Teacher:** [**how many**   ] (0) [**of these**] **does the** (0)

780. **Reijo:**   [oh where]

781. **Teacher:** **horsefly have** (0) **wings**.

782. **Keijo:**   aha. (0) [**yes**]

783. **Teacher:**   [and] then number three how

784. **Teacher:** [deep can the sperm whale] [dive-   ]

785. **Keijo:**   [**no I'm doing number one**]

786. **Reijo:**   [**oh seven**   ]

787. **Teacher:** and that's kaskelotti-(0) then you guess,

788. **Teacher:** what you think [is right   ]

789. **Reijo:**   [**sperm whale.**] (=literal translation)

790. **Ps:**   [((laughter))   ]

791. **Teacher:** [how many species of insects] are there

792. **Teacher:** in the world today. (0) **how many** (0)

793. **Teacher:** **species of insects are there in the world.**=

794. **Reijo:** =<u>over ten mi a millon.</u>

795. **Teacher:** mm-h-

796. **Keijo:** [mi a <u>million</u>   ]

797. **Veijo:** [couple   couple two millions]

In Excerpt 2, the main focus is on answering Questions 5 (*How many humps does a dromedary have?*) and 6 (*Where do tigers live?*):

Excerpt 2

884. **Irja:**   **what's number six**=

885. **P:**   =(x[xx   ]

886. **Keijo:**   [ove:r]

887. **P:**   [(xxx)]

888. **PF:**   [(xx)]

889. **Teacher:** **[for real]**

890. **PM:**   [(xxx)   ]

891. **Reijo:** <u>HUM</u>[<u>PS</u>] **WHAT: IS** <u>HUMP.</u>=

892. **Keijo:**   [(xx)]

893. **P:**   =[(xx).   ]

894. **PF:**   **[I'm not even** (x][xx]

895. **Reijo:**   **[OH YEAH,** <u>humps</u>]

896. **Reijo:** **yes [(indeed)]**

923. **Teijo:** **[how many (b)umps does a** (0) **dromedary [have]**

924. **Arja:**   **[wh]at is the**
                                          beast.=

925. **Teacher:** =mm.

926. **Reijo:** **[BUT THEY DO] LIVE [EVERYWHERE.]**

927. **Erja:**   [what-   ]

928. **Arja:**   [what is the beast   ]

929. **Reijo:**   TIGERS LIVE IN FINLAND AS WELL=

930. **Arja:**   =no I mean the <u>bat</u>

931. **Veijo:**   yeah in a zoo.

932. **Reijo:**   >yeah<=

933. **?:**   =[m[m   ]

934. **Erja:**   [I don't [know   ]

935. **Teacher:**   [(but as wild)]=

936. **PM:**   =yeah [(yes) in general (xx[x)   ]

937. **PM:**   [(xx[x)   ]

938. **Reijo:**   [in Africa and in Asia]

939. **Reijo:**   [do they live in both.]

940. **PF:**   [((laughs))   ]=

941. **Veijo:**   =(x) in Asia.

942. **Arja:**   wh-[what's this   ]

943. **Reijo:**   [well in Asia at least] (xx) the Siberian [tiger]

944. **P:**   [(x]x)=

When reporting on our analysis of the entire activity, we shall make use of these excerpts to illustrate more general points.

Findings: Situated constructions of literacy

Our concern was reading and writing, or a literacy event, within one specific activity in the EFL classroom. As mentioned, the textbook exercise was in the form of a quiz which would give the pupils an opportunity to practise listening comprehension. However, before listening and even while listening to the tape, the teacher and the pupils also did some reading and writing. Both of these, in turn, engaged the class in talk related to the text in the EFL textbook.

Within this activity, two constructions of literacy emerge from the talk (and action) in the EFL classroom. One type of literacy is imposed by the teacher on the rest of the class, being constructed through talk *about* text. The other type of literacy is established and maintained by some of the pupils through talk *around* text. These two types of talk differ in their form and focus but, more importantly, in each case reading and writing seem to take on different meanings.

Teacher-imposed literacy

The first type of literacy is established and maintained for the most part by the teacher. This construction of literacy stresses a number of points. First of all, the reading and writing within this activity are a means for the teacher to synchronise the group by making all pupils perform a school task simultaneously. Secondly, the activity stresses individual work on the part of the pupils: group work and negotiation among the pupils are discouraged. Thirdly, in working on the text, the focus is on form: the task is a matter of decoding the 10 questions, and copying one of the three answer alternatives in each pupil's notebook based on his/her own best guess. Finally, the number of right guesses is emphasised.

This construction of literacy is established through the teacher's talk (and partly through her action) in the classroom. The talk is closely tied to the text and activity at hand. We refer to this as talk *about* text (cf. Maybin & Moss, 1993). Talk *about* text can be of two types: *metalanguage* talk or *metatask* talk (both terms adapted from Hancock, 1997). Here, the *metalanguage* talk focuses on the linguistic form of the 10 questions, and it is typically in the form of monologue (van Lier, 1996). The teacher first reads out loud one question at a time and then provides the pupils with translations of some individual words or the full sentence (as in lines 763–781, 783–787 and 791–793 of Excerpt 1). Occasionally the teacher refers to and/or points at an English–Finnish word list in the textbook (as in line 765 of Excerpt 1 and in line 895 of Excerpt 2). In this way, the questions get eventually decoded. Interestingly, the teacher does this only with the first eight questions, after which she says, *and so on.* In other words, she seems to be providing the students with a model of how they should process the questions and make use of the word list. In contrast, the teacher makes no attempt to decode the answers. The only remark that she makes about the answer alternatives is that choosing them is a matter of guessing, which she repeats several times (as in lines 766, 771 and 787 of Excerpt 1).

The *metatask* talk is also from teacher to class or to individual pupils, and is concerned with performing the task. The teacher informs members of the class which teaching material they should have at hand, or which page, exercise or item she expects them to be working on. This talk is often accompanied with the teacher pointing at a relevant section in her own textbook or in those of the pupils'.

In these ways, the first type of literacy gets established and several attempts are made by the teacher in the course of the activity to maintain it either through talk *about* text, or combined with action in the classroom. Consider Excerpt 1 first. From line 769 onwards, some of the boys are discussing amongst themselves how many wings a horsefly has. The teacher interferes by saying *put your own an-guess in the notebook.* At the same time, she is pointing at Reijo, one of the boys. Thus she comes to stress that the pupils should be working on their own. The message is the same in Excerpt 2 from line 891 onwards: Reijo is wondering, *humps **what is** hump*, mispronouncing the key word. The teacher responds by pointing at the English–Finnish word list in the pupil's textbook. Furthermore, consider Excerpt 2 from line 926 onwards. Reijo opens up a discussion about the whereabouts of tigers, ***but they do live everywhere*** (raising his voice), which is not one of the three alternatives suggested in the textbook (for details, see Appendix 2). The discussion continues among some of the boys. Once again, the teacher interferes by remarking ***but as wild***. In other words, she insists on a close reading of the text at hand. Accordingly, the pupils are supposed to choose one out of the three alternatives provided in the textbook; they are not expected to come up with answers from their own reasoning.

As for the pupils, they can either comply with the literacy imposed on them by the teacher, or alternatively they can challenge it (see below). Compliance is accomplished through talk *about* text of two types. First, there is *metalanguage* talk that is initiated by a pupil and either addressed to the teacher or to fellow pupils. It comprises appeals for translations of individual words (see lines 775 of Excerpt 1, and lines 884, 891, 923 and 927–940 of Excerpt 2, where Erja and Arja, two girls, are discussing the meaning of the word *bat,* which Arja has first misread as *beast, **what is** the beast*) or full sentences (see lines 775 and 776–777 of Excerpt 1, and line 884 of Excerpt 2, where Irja asks Arja, sitting next to her, in Finnish, ***what's number six***). Or the pupils discuss amongst themselves which of the three answer alternatives to choose. Consider, for example, lines 768–772 of Excerpt 1. There, some of the boys are considering whether a horsefly has two or four wings. The third alternative, six wings, is not discussed at all.

Secondly, there is also *metatask* talk initiated by the pupils: they wish to inform or inquire of the teacher, in particular, where they are in processing the text. For example, in line 785 of Excerpt 1 Keijo remarks, ***no, I'm doing number one***. He is lagging behind as the teacher is already commenting on Question 3. At the same time, this is a way for the pupil to show the teacher that he is with her, busy working on the exercise even though at his own pace.

To sum up, the first construction of literacy stresses a superficial processing of the text. It is of importance to complete the school task in a fast and efficient way with little personal involvement on the part of the participants. In comparison, the second construction of literacy emerging within the activity stresses other points, with reading and writing taking on different meanings.

Student-imposed literacy

As mentioned, attempts are also made by the pupils to challenge the first type of literacy although not all the pupils get involved in this. In their challenging they come to establish and maintain literacy of another type. Unlike teacher-imposed literacy, student-imposed literacy emerges covertly, bit by bit, in interactions among some of the boys.

Student-imposed literacy differs from teacher-imposed literacy in a number of respects. Firstly, the boys see the work around the piece of written text at hand as a group effort. They want to negotiate the answers with each other, and thus come to resist the idea of individual work emphasised by the teacher. Secondly, these pupils do not want to perform the task in a superficial way. They are not happy with simply decoding the text: for them the questions and answers have real subject matter worth talking about. Thirdly, the pupils do not like the idea of guessing; they want to answer the questions on the basis of their general knowledge of animals. Fourthly, these pupils see their group effort and negotiation around the piece of written text as entertainment, and by joking and playing with words they can show solidarity towards each other.

Student-imposed literacy is constructed through talk *around* text. By this we mean talk that somehow goes beyond the text and activity at hand to the world outside the classroom. This talk takes place among pupils only; the teacher is either excluded or she does not want to be involved in it. Talk *around* text focuses on the answers, more specifically, on their contents rather than the given alternatives. In negotiating the answers the pupils often draw on contexts outside the immediate setting by resorting to their own world knowledge concerning, e.g. the Siberian tiger, or by referring to other texts, such as magazines they have read or TV programmes they have seen. This talk among the boys can be characterised as conversation as opposed to the monologue typical of teacher-imposed literacy (see van Lier, 1996). A good example of this kind of talk can be found in lines 926–944 of Excerpt 2. First, Reijo opens the discussion and challenges Question 6 about tigers and all three answer alternatives (for details, see Appendix 2) by remarking that tigers live everywhere, *in Finland as well*. Veijo agrees, *yeah in a zoo*. The teacher, in turn, challenges the boys, by limiting the discussion to wild tigers and thus pointing out that they have to choose from among the alternatives in the textbook. Reijo is still not happy and he goes on considering the last two answer alternatives, Africa and Asia, with Veijo. Reijo wonders, *could they live in both*, whereas Veijo argues that they live in Asia. Finally, Reijo resorts to his own knowledge about Siberian tigers, settling eventually for the third alternative, that is, that tigers live in Asia.

In addition, talk *around* text promotes solidarity among the pupils. This is achieved by joking and playing with words, for instance. In this way, the pupils also challenge the first type of literacy imposed on them by the teacher. First, consider lines 783–790 of Excerpt 1. The teacher is reading aloud Question 3 concerning sperm whales. This species translates into Finnish as *kaskelotti*. The word has nothing to do with sperm but Reijo uses the literal translation *sperma-valas* (sperma = sperm, valas = whale), which is followed by laughter: the other pupils find it extremely funny. The teacher, however, ignores the joke. Another example of playing with words can be found in line 923 of Excerpt 2. Teijo changes the first sound of the Finnish word *kyttyrä* (= hump), turning it into *hyttyrä,* which is a word that cannot be found in a dictionary but which still carries some meaning. This is almost like changing *humps* into *bumps* in English.

In summary, by establishing and maintaining a second type of literacy, and at the same time challenging the official agenda of the EFL lesson pursued by the teacher, some of the pupils give us a glimpse of how they make sense of literacy in the EFL classroom. They resist the superficial and efficient completion of a school task, refuse to work on their own and are dissatisfied with decoding and guessing. They would rather see the task as a meaningful group effort which relates to their world and which is also entertaining. Nevertheless, even these pupils acknowledge teacher-imposed literacy, switching from one literacy to another, from their world to the teacher's world, and back again in the course of the EFL activity.

Conclusion

The focus of our study was the constructions of literacy through talk (and action) surrounding a piece of written text. More specifically, we looked at a literacy event within a specific activity during an EFL lesson, involving year 7 secondary pupils. Importantly, the activity was not officially defined as a reading/writing event. In this respect, our study differs in its focus from some previous ones, conducted in L1 contexts (e.g. Bloome 1993, 1994; Maybin & Moss, 1993; Moss, 1998).

At least two types of literacy seem to emerge from the interaction (and action) in the EFL classroom. The first type of literacy was constructed through talk *about* text, both *metalanguage* and *metatask* talk. Either the text or the task were commented on by the teacher or the pupils with the text under close scrutiny. For the teacher, it was important to get the school activity completed in a fast and efficient way. This compares with procedural display observed in Bloome's (1994) study on L1 literacy. At the same time, this activity provided the pupils with opportunities to show good studentship, as was the case also in a number of studies on L1 literacies (e.g. Bloome, 1993, 1994; Maybin & Moss, 1993). In other words, with talk *about* text the pupils could show the teacher that they were busy completing the listening comprehension exercise.

However, some of the pupils came to challenge teacher-imposed literacy by making attempts to establish and maintain literacy of a second type. Student-imposed literacy was constructed through talk *around* text. In other words, this literacy went beyond decoding the questions and guessing the right answers. References were made by the pupils to their own knowledge of various species of animals and/or to other texts as sources of information before choosing answer alternatives. The pupils also had a good time, e.g. by joking amongst themselves. Interestingly, the teacher allowed all this to take place in the class, but she did not take part in it herself. In our opinion, this can be interpreted in two ways: she either challenges the second type of literacy by ignoring it, or she complies with the group of pupils by allowing their literacy to develop up to a point.

Two further points deserve mention. In earlier studies (e.g. Bloome 1993, 1994; Maybin & Moss, 1993; Moss, 1998), the constructions of L1 literacy in educational settings have been found to vary from one event to another but not necessarily within one event. In our study of L2 literacy, the latter was indeed the case in the classroom. Second, it is important to stress that the constructions of literacy within this activity were by no means stable ones. There was a constant struggle between the two types of literacy, and some of the pupils moved from one literacy to another, and back again. A group of boys, especially, challenged the literacy imposed on them right from the beginning of the activity. It was only every now and then that they complied with the teacher's agenda in the EFL classroom. The second type of literacy established by the pupils was not, however, strong enough to overcome the first type. As a matter of fact, in the third stage of the activity the whole group ends up complying with the teacher's construction of literacy: one by one the pupils report to the teacher on how many answers they have got right. The dominance of the first type of literacy can be explained by the asymmetry of power relations between the teacher and the pupils in the classroom. To sum up, our study provides evidence for the multiplicity and variability of literacy in the EFL classroom.

The classroom is an extremely complex setting involving not only the participants and activities but also the resources the participants draw on. So far, we have mainly concentrated on the interaction between the participants (and action) around a piece of text. However, we acknowledge the important role that resources play in the construction of literacies in complementing the interaction and in constraining the activities in the EFL classroom. In the future, we intend to pursue this issue further by addressing, for example, the relationship between power and access to resources in shaping the constructions of literacy in the L2 classroom.

Appendix 1: Transcription conventions

[ ]	overlapping speech
(1), (2)	length of a pause in seconds
(0)	untimed pause, less than one second
text=	
=text2	latching speech
CAPITALS	loud speech
°high circles°	soft speech
<slow>	slow speech
>fast<	fast speech
shadow	emphatic stress
exte:nsio::n	noticeable extension of the sound or syllable with the colon
cut off wo-	cut off word or sentence
.	falling intonation
-	rising intonation
,	continuing intonation
marked	marked pronunciation
mispronounced	mispronounced
((laughs))	comments
(x)	incomprehensible item, probably one word only
(xx)	incomprehensible item of phrase length
(xxx)	incomprehensible item beyond phrase length
•laughing•	laughing production of an utterance
((x))	incomprehensible sound
((xx))	incomprehensible sounds
singing	singing production of an utterance

Appendix 2: Animal Quiz

LISTEN   LISTEN   LISTEN   LISTEN

ANIMAL QUIZ

Before you listen to the quiz, try and answer the questions below.

Then listen and check if you were right.

1. How many bones does a giraffe have in its neck?	7 / 17 / 27
2. How many wings does a horsefly have?	two / four / six
3. How deep can the sperm whale dive?	1,000 m / 2,000m / 3,000m
4. How many species of insects are there in the world today?	over 1,000 / over a million / over 10 million
5. How many humps does a dromedary have?	one / two / three
6. Where do tigers live?	South America / Africa / Asia
7. Which animal lives upside down?	the bat / the sloth / the vampire
8. How fast can the cheetah run?	60 km/h / 80 km/h / 100 km/h
9. How far can a sloth move in one minute?	1 metre / 3 metres / 6 metres
10. In which coutnry do giant pandas live?	India / China / Japan

Make up your own questions and ask the class.

Westlake, P. *et al.* (1995) *The News Headlines. Courses 1–4* (p. 54). Porvoo: WSOY.

References

Baker, C. and Freebody, P. (1989) *Children's First School Books*. Oxford: Blackwell.

Barton, D. (1994) *Literacy: An introduction to the ecology of written language.* Oxford: Blackwell.

Barton, D. and Hamilton, M. (1998) *Local Literacies: Reading and writing in one community.* London: Routledge.

Baynham, M. (1995) *Literacy Practices: Investigating literacy in social contexts.* London: Longman.

Bloome, D. (1989) Beyond access: An ethnographic study of reading and writing in a seventh grade classroom. In D. Bloome (ed.) *Classrooms and Literacy* (pp. 53–104). Norwood, NJ: Ablex.

Bloome, D. (1993) Necessary indeterminacy and the microethnographic study of reading as a social process. *Journal of Research in Reading* 16, 98–111.

Bloome, D. (1994) Reading as a social process in a middle school classroom. In D. Graddol, J. Maybin and B. Stierer (eds) *Researching Language and Literacy in Social Context* (pp. 100–30). Clevedon: Multilingual Matters.

Bloome, D. and Green, J. L. (1992). Educational contexts of literacy. *Annual Review of Applied Linguistics* 12, 49–70.

Gee, J. P. (1996) *Social Linguistics and Literacies: Ideology in discourses* (2nd edn). Exeter: Taylor & Francis.

Gregory, E. (1994) Negotiation as a criterial factor in learning to read in a second language. In D. Graddol, J. Maybin and B. Stierer (eds) *Researching Language and Literacy in Social Context* (pp. 49–61). Clevedon: Multilingual Matters.

Hancock, M. (1997) Behind classroom code switching: Layering and language choice in L2 learner interaction. *TESOL Quarterly* 31, 217–35.

Heath, S. B. (1983) *Ways with Words: Language, life, and work in communities and classrooms*. Cambridge: Cambridge University Press.

Maybin, J. and Moss, G. (1993) Talk about texts: Reading as a social event. *Journal of Research in Reading* 16, 138–47.

Moss, G. (1998) Analysing literacy events: Mapping gendered configurations of readers, texts and contexts. Poster at the Annual Meeting of BAAL, September 1998.

Street, B. V. (1984) *Literacy in Theory and Practice*. Cambridge: Cambridge University Press.

Street, B. V. (1995) Social Literacies: Critical approaches to literacy in development, *Ethnography and Education*. London: Longman.

van Lier, L. (1996) *Interaction in the Language Curriculum: Awareness, autonomy and authenticity*. London: Longman.

Wells, G. (1990) Talk about text: Where literacy is learned and taught. *Curriculum Inquiry* 20, 369–405.

Westlake, P. *et al.* (1995) *The News Headlines*. Porvoo: WSOY.

5 Critical Literacy as Classroom Interaction

CATHERINE WALLACE

Institute of Education, University of London

Abstract

This paper explores the notion of critical literacy as a classroom project. It argues that classroom based critical literacy which takes a critical discourse analysis perspective is supported and strengthened by critical talk. Critical talk is defined, for the purposes of this paper, as having the following features: it offers distance on present attitudes and beliefs; it is discursive and exploratory rather than affective; it is mutually constructed in the classroom community. The second half of the paper considers ways in which the teacher's execution of one of the key speech acts, typically in her gift, *reformulation,* serves to facilitate or frustrate the development of critical talk in the support of classroom-based critical literacy.

Introduction

My aim in this paper is to explore the notion of critical literacy as a classroom project. In doing so, I shall make reference to a course, *Critical Reading,* which I taught to advanced learners of English as a foreign language. The class was centred on text analysis of the kind familiar in Critical Discourse Analysis procedures (cf., e.g. Fairclough, 1989; Wallace, 1992). This paper looks at the negotiated interpretations by teacher and students, mediated by critical talk, which followed the text analysis. I shall consider what we might mean by critical talk, before going on to look at the teacher's role in the facilitation of such talk, focusing, for illustrative purposes, on *reformulation.* First, though, in what ways do we want to use the term *critical*?

Critical Literacy and Power

Despite the difficulty in the acknowledged overuse of the term critical (cf., e.g. Lankshear, 1994) a link with power seems a key strand in much commentary: in CDA approaches this relates to the ways in which power relations are played out within texts – as the object of study in *critical reading* courses – but also within the classroom itself between teacher and students. In talking of power one should be careful, however, not to assume merely malign effects. As Reynolds (1990), drawing on Giddens' interpretation of power, notes, power may be taken to refer to relations of domination/subjugation, illegitimately exercised; but power can also be seen, especially as a collaborative project, as 'transformative capacity' in Giddens' terms (cf. Cassell, 1993: 227), that is a positive use of shared resources to achieve outcomes. Moreover, power as transformative capacity is promoted in the classroom by the judicious and legitimate exercise of authority by the teacher. This is evident in the manner in which the teacher ensures equality of opportunity for class participants to take the floor in discussion and offers adequate access to knowledge and understanding. The legitimate exercise of teacher authority is actively empowering, helping to fulfil transformative potential by establishing the territory on which all class participants can become, in Goffman's terms, *authors* of the opinions and judgements expressed, as opposed to mere *animators* of them as when required to activate prescribed roles and syllabuses (Goffman, 1981). As authors, students and teacher can lay claim to a stronger degree of reciprocity than is typical of classroom talk, bringing it closer to *constative speech* in Habermas's (1984) terms, where the focus is on the unimpeded articulation, exchange and defence of ideas. If we accept both the desirability of mutually authored constative speech in classroom settings and the necessity for the teacher's management of debate, a major question to be addressed becomes: when does authority, as legitimately exercised in support of mutual empowerment, slip into dominative power which is disruptive of the kind of enquiry which best supports the development of critical literacy?

Critical Literacy and Critical Talk

Critical literacy comes into play not just in the multilayered awareness and interpretation of texts but in talk around texts. For learner readers talk around texts has long been acknowledged to be key to fuller understandings of written texts. Wells (1991), for instance, notes the role of 'epistemic literacy', by which young childrens' interpretative activity is enriched by exploratory talk usually with an adult; where textual meaning is treated not as fixed and autonomous, but as open to negotiation. Also with mature readers, talk directs future reading and aids rethinking of texts already read. In this sense it is part of an ongoing critical process. Moreover, talk can be said to be critical to the extent that it deals not merely with ideas, but is interpersonally constructed in interpretations of texts which challenge everyday convergent readings. I shall argue below that the role of talk in a CDA-inspired Critical Literacy class may be characterised by three distinctive features:

- critical talk offers distance on one's own feelings, views and beliefs rather than articulating involvement with them;

- critical talk is expository and exploratory rather than affirmative of feelings or established beliefs;

- critical talk is co-authored and oriented to mutual empowerment.

Critical Talk as the Achievement of Distance

Some teaching approaches which go by the name of *critical*, e.g. Kanpol (1994), emphasise personal development and empathy – involvement rather than the attempt to gain some critical distance from one's own current or previous beliefs or practices. My concern in the *Critical Reading* class was not personal empowerment but social analysis; not to celebrate difference or diversity in itself, but to examine and challenge the bases of claimed difference; not to take a relativist position which encourages the equal valuing of diverse cultural practices but to be prepared to censure practices typical of either one's own cultural milieu or that of others. Some versions of critical pedagogy – necessarily linked to critical literacy as a practical project – involve the romanticising, or exoticising of the remote or unfamiliar on the one hand or, on the other, the celebration of one's own identity, especially where students are perceived to be at high risk in terms of self esteem. My view is that the transformative capacity of critical literacy cannot be realised without a continuing, sometimes uncomfortable, process of critique and *metacritique*. By metacritique I mean the ability and willingness not just to undertake text analysis in the first instance, but to stand back from previous critique, to revisit earlier judgements from some distance of time and place. What is involved is the development, collaboratively achieved in the critical literacy classroom, of, as Hasan (1998: 53) describes it, 'a discursive ability which can turn back to reflect on discourse itself'. In this, critical literacy is close not just, as noted earlier, to 'epistemic' literacy, but to what Hasan terms 'reflective literacy'. Hasan sees the priorities of 'reflective' literacy as 'reflection, enquiry and analysis'. Related to a practical pedagogy, this can be translated into: reflection on texts and our own readings of texts; shared enquiry with others and close analysis of specific textual features.

Critical Talk as Constative Speech

One goal in the *Critical Reading* class was to promote discursive or constative speech, in the Habermasian spirit that a goal of rationally agreed interpretations of events or texts, or rationally based agreement to disagree, can be negotiated, though this is not to say that 'interpretations must lead in every case to a stable and unambiguously differentiated argument' (Habermas, 1984: 100). In other words, consensus is possible and progress feasible – if not in the sense of reaching absolute goals as suggested by 'right' and 'wrong' answers, then towards more adequate 'truthful' interpretations. In claiming this, I part company from those such as Pennycook (1994b: 131), who, dispensing with notions of truth and truthfulness, have taken a postmodern Foucauldian turn in their proposals for a critical pedagogy.

Critical Talk as Mutual Empowerment

Dominative power in the hands or either teacher or students might be seen as *strategic* in Habermas's terms (Habermas, 1984). The teacher may be using her role to assert power rather than exercise authority – to proclaim her status; in Goffman's terms, she is *animating* her role as the teacher, playing out 'what teachers do', not, that is, contributing substantively as *author* to the development of knowledge or debate within the classroom community. On her part, the student may be asserting power to disrupt or challenge the teacher's position. Moreover, both teacher and students may, rather than building critical co-authored understanding, be **arguing** strategically, adversarily, point-scoring, delivering the rhetorical goods. Indeed this is sometimes said to be what **argument** is. I would wish it rather to be seen in Kress's words as an 'institutionally recognisable way of handling difference' (Kress, 1989: 12). In this view, argument provides the means for the production of texts constituted in difference, not as necessarily persuasive, or oppositional, but as a way of acknowledging the existence of a range of perspectives, through talk which is collaborative rather than dominative and strategic.

How can we in practical ways aim to nurture these features of critical talk in the classroom? How can we ensure the achievement of critical distance, the promotion of discursive, constative rather than affective speech and of collaborative rather than dominative power? I exemplify below from the *Critical Reading* class. The students who feature in the episodes quoted are: Yukako from Japan, Virginia, Blanca and Domingo from Spain, and Sylvie and Sylvain from France. All were undergraduate or Cambridge Proficiency students at Thames Valley University where I taught the class which met weekly for two hours over a 14 week period.

Promoting distance

We can aid reflection and distance by adjusting the mode of enquiry. In a critically oriented classroom the everyday is reconsidered, reread and recontextualised. In a *Critical Reading* class everyday texts such as news articles, flyers and ads are favoured; the aim is not however to read such texts in everyday, essentially co-operative, kinds of ways so much as to read against the grain of perceived common sense. We can also allow opportunities for 'standing back' and reflecting subsequently on what has happened in the classroom community itself. In the *Critical Reading* course, private, relatively unconsidered reading in preparation for the class was revisited in the classroom group text analysis sessions which were then further reconsidered in the public plenary classroom discussion. Here representatives were expected to report differences, tensions and consensus within their group. Indeed part of the development of critical talk was seen to be the bringing in of reference to other points of view. The first private reading was likely to be a relatively convergent or co-operative one, with resistance of various kinds emerging at later stages as readers were able to pool their contributions from different cultural perspectives, and to take on board alternative views. Following each lesson students were expected to record and comment in diaries on textual interpretations and the accompanying classroom talk.

Three months after the course, follow-up interviews further allowed for a metacritical stance, where students and teacher might reflect on earlier responses. Adjustments of mode necessitate adjustment of code: asked to comment at some distance of time and space from the original episode where a text was discussed, students are forced to elaborate and specify. Thus Virginia comments in her follow up interview:

Do you remember the Spanish text talking about the waiter – the text of the tourist – Englishman who went to Spain, the one we were discussing? The first lines of the article were the description of the guy and his mother and what he did on Saturdays and his girlfriend and then, once you have presented and introduced the person, then you can tell the story. It's very personalised – very … They always look for an example and he and he and he and he did that and something happened to him and its everywhere, in the news, in the radio … You think it's natural but it was new for me … It drew my attention … You need proofs in general … in British newspapers everything's got its name and surname and age and … Even when they go to Rwanda … And they interview a person and they always give the name. Who cares what's the name, the important thing is the opinion – they (the British readers) become aware of the importance of the event when they've got someone who has suffered the event and is telling it. It's because its very important, individualism, here.

Here Virginia does not just relate back to a single key text studied in class; she explores the implications of the earlier analysis for other exemplars of the newspaper genre and other modes subsequently observed, such as radio. She relates the specific reading to a context of wider generalisation. In Lankshear's words (Lankshear, 1994: 10) she is able to 'make a critical reading of ... social practices ... which are made possible and partially sustained through the reading of texts'. She shows a metacritical stance in short.

Promoting the language of enquiry

A second goal of the *Critical Reading* course was the promotion of the language of argument, of intellectual enquiry, the kind of talk where opinions are not merely stated but logically substantiated, through illustration and supporting statements, where ideas rather than experiences are exchanged, or rather personal experiences are articulated within the context of wider social implications. Students need a language to engage in metalevel talk about texts and classroom processes, to move their commentary beyond the immediate, personal and contingent. In connection with this expectation we might compare transcripts (a) and (b) below. In (a), the teacher asks why his Year 10 secondary school students laughed during the screening of romantic scenes in *Romeo and Juliet*.

Transcript (a)

Student A: It was so funny

Teacher: Okay, why did you find it funny, though?

Student B: It was so stupid.

Students: Yeah

Teacher: What was stupid about it? Why did you think it was stupid?

Student C: They were so serious and so old-fashioned.

Student D: Yeah. They were so lovey-dovey.

Teacher: All right, if you were Romeo and Juliet, then, how would you be talking to each other?

Student E: The difference in our talk –

Student C: Nobody shows their emotions like that much any more.

Teacher: So you don't think that sort of open display of emotions is something that –

Student C: Nowadays, if people, like, show that much emotion, they get all worried that the other person will think, well, hey, they need me that much, I can just treat them how I want; they'll always be there

(from Morgan, 1997: 127)

In (b), the student Sylvie from the *Critical Reading* course is giving her views on a text about the release of Nelson Mandela from prison (cf. Appendix: text 4):

Transcript (b)

> The headline shocked me because 'Whites Out'. For me it's a reference to something against blacks. In fact, because ... It could say 'Blacks Out' and it will, would have been a racist headline and it's very shocking because ... I think that this article is racist – really, because of the title, because erm ... Whites yes whites shot dead as Nelson says: 'Keep up struggle' and 'whites were terrorised as young blacks er celebrated Nelson Mandela's release' All faults are put on black people. I think you can say that, you can say that it's racist.

In transcript (a) the students comment experientially without elaborating. Even though the teacher in (a) specifically *invites* hypothesis in 'if you were Romeo and Juliet', the students continue to offer narrative responses, close to their immediate experience. Sylvie, in (b), on the other hand, sees the need to justify the nature of her response. The field of discourse is public and elaborated. Although, as a non-native speaker, she struggles to find the correct unreal conditional tense, saying 'It could say' as opposed to 'it could have said', Sylvie is honouring the expectation that if the goal is intellectual enquiry – constative speech in Habermas's terms – then participants will be expected to offer supports to points of view, justifications for claims put forward and to distance themselves from the here and now, as Sylvie does through hypothesis. She does this without solicitation by the teacher. Indeed, I as the teacher can take little credit for the nature of Sylvie's response. It is likely that she has drawn on her prior educational experience to activate the principle of elaborated, critical talk.

Promoting collaborative talk

What kind of interpersonal behaviour on the part of teacher and students is conducive to the promotion of critical literacy? How can one promote collaborative over strategic talk? Both Peled & Blum-Kulka (1998) and Allwright (1996) talk of the 'social text' in order to account for the motivation of much classroom interaction as primarily phatic, concerned with what Allwright calls simply 'getting along'. Allwright sees the social and pedagogic text in opposition, with the social – the 'getting along' – in some cases replacing the pedagogic text – the 'getting on', and this is a characteristic of some so-called communicative classrooms which have strongly favoured casual conversation over other speech styles. However, the social and the pedagogic need not be seen as competing over territory: rather we might consider how best to use the 'getting along' in order to 'get on'. In other words the social text should facilitate the pedagogic one, not substitute for it. Arguably this can be seen in those cases where students are, both in a spirit of solidarity and in honouring critical talk as a collaborative project, making reference to their partner's observation. Here is an example from Virginia:

> In the rest of the texts he's the subject – he walks to freedom or walks out of prison or – he's the subject and there's one interesting point that Sylvie noticed: in the first text the rest of the participants are accompanied by the possessive – his followers, his African National Congress ... all the violent participants are related to Mandela explicitly.

The Teacher's Role in the Support of Critical Talk

One difficulty in creating a congenial classroom environment supportive of critical talk is that even in classes of adults, classroom interaction is necessarily an unequal encounter, with the teacher as overall manager of events. The question then is, given the teacher's legitimate managerial role, what spaces can be opened up to facilitate critical enquiry around texts in the classroom? How can we ensure as much reciprocity as possible? Classrooms with apparent richness of different contributions may nonetheless be monologic, in that as Peled & Blum-Kulka (1998: 2) note, learner contributions merely reproduce the teacher text. This is the difficulty with simply looking quantitatively at features of classroom discourse. Conversely, teacher monologue in the literal sense can be dialogic to the extent that it is oriented to mutual understanding. Its rhetorical style may be interactive in that it prompts the raising of questions in the course of monologue. In the former case, where the teacher is requiring the students to reproduce her own text, we might say that in Goffman's terms the teacher is merely *animating* her role. She is playing out *what teachers do*. Below is an example of myself playing out teacher behaviour in a lesson fairly near the beginning of the *Critical Reading* course.

Domingo: I believe that the whole advertisement doesn't make sense at all ... Yeah. And I think that they do that on purpose. I think they do that on purpose because that way

Virginia: It does. It makes sense

Blanca: It makes sense

Domingo: It makes sense? The whole thing?

Virginia: It makes sense. Yes Very clear

CW: Christine?

Virginia: No, Virginia, Virginia

CW: Oh Virginia I meant Virginia yes Virginia

Domingo: I wish everybody could explain to me, you know

CW: Virginia, okay, Virginia thinks it does make sense ...

Virginia: yes it does

CW: so would you like to say what the sense is?

In this series of exchanges, I am intervening with a display of power –
'snatching a turn' from a student as Reynolds (1990: 125) puts it – unnecessarily
brokering the main exchange between Virginia and Domingo and adding nothing
to support either the pedagogic or social text. At this point legitimate managerial
control has slipped into power of the dominative kind. On another occasion,
however, similar behaviour might be interpreted as a legitimate intervention to
ensure fair turns. For these reasons, it is less interesting merely to quantify the
familiar classroom moves in the gift of the teacher, for example reformulation,
feedback and praise than to look at **how** they are interpreted. In the rest of this
paper I shall look at the teacher's management of reformulation in some representative episodes of the *Critical Reading* class.

Power as Dominative or Collaborative: Focus on reformulation

I shall use the term 'reformulation' much as does Thomas (1984) to describe
unequal encounters where those with power summarise or bring together, meta-
pragamatically, the substance of what has been said. Thomas draws her examples
from police data where clear lines of authority make on-record responses more
likely on the part of superiors. Classrooms will vary: while teachers of young
children are likely to be on-record for much of the time, with adult students there
are stronger expectations to attend to the social text – to address face wants and
needs for instance by mitigating directness. It follows that teachers of adults can
afford to weaken – or make less explicit – the managerial aspects of their role
and that we might expect greater variation in the execution of reformulation.
Reformulation may take on varying kinds of significance in the overall discourse:
it may for instance, simply animate what students have already contributed or it
may, more creatively and productively, bring together several points of view.
Finally, reformulations may, in some cases, be jointly produced by teacher and

students, becoming in the process less like acts which provide closure articulated from a position of dominative power than ongoing restatements or reconsiderations of positions, more typical of constative speech.

The examples below are selected from one kind of classroom episode, which is the feedback one where students present their text analyses, prepared within their groups, to the whole class. Within this feedback episode, teacher reformulation tends to occur at particular junctures, particularly when attention moves from one pair or group to the next. In order to shed light on the wider question as to how the teacher might progress from the exercise of individual dominative power towards a more power*ful*, jointly negotiated interaction, facilitative of the development of critical literacy, I shall look at some examples of the management of *reformulation* in three classroom episodes, one near the beginning of the course, one in the middle and one in the penultimate class.

Three Classroom Episodes

(1) Power and Control

This was a readership awareness task given at week four of the course: Students were asked to consider who a car advertisement (Text 1: picture plus technical text) was addressed to.

Example 1

1. **CW:** And men can understand more difficult language, you think?

2. **Blanca:** (Laughs) No, I don't think so but they may think so

3. **CW:** Yes, this came up, I think in that in ...

4. **Blanca:** Especially compared with ...

5. **CW:** Yes, when you look at the other one (another advertisement) – that makes the contrast doesn't it? I think some of you had the chance to look at this one, which is, you can see, clearly for women – the heart shape and so on. **So we've got an educated reader, em, somebody with political and economic power, and male.** Right, let's move on and see if we can ... thank you very much, that's good ... eh Domingo

Blanca's attempts to engage in a jointly constructed summary of the argument by initiating reference to a contrasting text is frustrated. In two succeeding overlapping turns (2/3 and 4/5) I prevail over Blanca and go on, briskly and routinely, to reformulate the students' main observations about the key text in bullet point manner: *educated reader; political and economic power; male.* I then explicitly signal closure and move on to the next group. I do little more than animate the students' words and my own managerial role, as evidenced by the cursory 'thanks' for the students' contribution.

Example 2

1. **CW (to Y):** You were saying ... she's shy (laughing) that you picked out some of the vocabulary that gave you the impression of a male reader?

2. **Y:** Oh yes, I thought especially the phrase, it says: A 16 valve 2 litre power plant with variable inlet manifold fuel-injection

3. **CW:** Yes, yes, you see its not just 'manifold fuel injection' It's that whole phrase isn't it? Its a whole noun clause, isn't it?: 'a 16 valve 2 litre power plant with variable inlet manifold fuel injection'. That's all one noun phrase.

Here I simply repeat Yukako's own observation, adding little new of substance apart from the confusing claim that the phrase beginning 'A 16 valve' – Yukako herself has already used the term 'phrase' – is both a Noun Phrase and a Noun Clause!

(2) Mandela

In this class, at week nine of the course, students were analysing a set of newspaper texts about Nelson Mandela's release. The language focus was on the field of discourse and, within that, on participants and processes.

Example 3

In this example I am summing up two competing interpretations of a text by Sylvain and Blanca.

1. **CW:** Thank you, that's interesting, you were taking slightly, well different views there, but you, that em..

2. **Sylvain:** especially the first one ...

3. **CW:** ... yes, that in a sense that, is he the sort of victim of events or is he ... I think **both** are true..

4. **General:** Yes, yes

5. **CW:** ... in a in a funny sort of way, eh oddly that ... be because texts can mean two things at the same time, let's remember that. There isn't you know, this is where language is so complex. Um so I know what Sylvain was saying, if I can come in, where it says, for instance, it talks about em, the release of Nelson Mandela, whereas what do the other texts say, did you notice? How do they describe ... yes?

There is evidence of a shift of tenor from the more classic teacher reformulating moves in earlier episodes. In turn 1 for instance there is a subtle but important shift in impact from a managerial 'good' as in example 1 or the 'yes, yes' in example 2 to the authored 'interesting'. The 'different views' of the students are genuinely felt to contribute to a richer – ambivalent – account of textual meaning. That my response shows a greater degree of on-line authorship is evidenced by the hesitancy of the discourse. The very fact that the students have not responded to any preset list of 'things to notice' in the text necessitates authored expression in my attempt at reformulation. At the same time I retain a tight managerial rein, disallowing Sylvain the opportunity to take over the role of reformulating the points made to date. He shows a preparedness to do so in turn 2. I half-acknowledge this turn stealing, with the later words in turn 5: 'if I can come in' thus signalling a belated awareness of my unnecessary intervention and a missed opportunity for more collaborative talk.

Example 4 (this exchange follows on from example 3)

1. **Virginia:** In the rest of the texts he's the subject – he 'walks to freedom' or 'walks out of prison' or ... He's the subject and there's one interesting point that Sylvie noticed: in the first text the rest of the participants are accompanied by the possessive: 'his followers'; 'his African National Congress Organisation' ... 'his release' so It's somehow blaming all the violence on Mandela, all the violent participants are related to Mandela explicitly.

2. **CW:** this is why I think both what Sylvain was saying is true and what (Blanca said). You know **both** those impressions were made because it's true: 'his followers' – all the way through the violence is associated with Mandela but at the same time he's not ... he's been made **powerless** er by because the opening subject is 'Violence and death disfigured the release of Nelson Mandela;' Good.

In turn 1, Virginia, having briefly responded to my request to consider the other texts, returns to text one offering further textual support for Blanca's earlier expressed view of the strong agency linked to Mandela in this text, acknowledging at the same time her partner Sylvie as the source of this observation. I accept this additional contribution, to strengthen and reinstate my previous reformulation of both Sylvain's and Blanca's ways of interpreting the linguistic choices in the text. In this way a number of students have been able to make a contribution to this reformulation.

(3) Childminder

This text, which was the major focus of week 13 of the course, related to the case of a childminder reprimanded by the local council for the possession of a golliwog. In example 5, Yukako is commenting on the ambiguity of the word *support* in the banner headline: *Support floods in for childminder who refuses to get rid of 'racist toy'*.

Example 5

1. **Y:**   Yes, er what we em found confusing is er a bit like em em support for ... what ... we are talking about? Is it well because, this Mrs Newton's attitude is not so clear, clearly said here, we don't know if she's a real racist or just doing her job as a childminder, we don't know that. And then it eh, we have to know that first. And this 'support' meaning's become a different meaning as well. Is it supporting her being racist or is it supporting her being a childmind, good childminder, we don't know yet

2. **CW:**   Thats very interesting. What evidence in the text is there for these positions do you think or why – lets put it differently – why is it ambiguous?

3. **V:**   She never says she's not racist. She never says that. I think she's so convinced of the way she's been brought up and everybody's been reading these stories for a long time er well maybe we're all racist and we don't realise. It's part of our consciousness

4. **CW:**   What is racist? This is the thing

5. **V:**   and maybe the council is trying to reject this and try to try to erm separate the concepts and tell you that this is racist. I don't know.

Here I have largely abandoned any clear reformulating or evaluative role. In turn 2, 'That's very interesting' for instance is a substantive response to Yukako's observation which relates to a textual ambiguity which I have not previously noticed. The game by which students align responses to teacher expectation, or 'Guess What Teacher Thinks' as it is sometimes known, is suspended. In the subsequent series of turns with Virginia there is a further shift in teacher role towards what Young (1992) calls 'fellow enquirer'. Questions are exploratory, being questions to which the teacher has no answer – indeed the questions are not readily answerable. This is certainly the spirit in which Virginia interprets the function of my questions in turns 2 and 4. She continues to build her own line of enquiry across her turns 3 and 5. The presence of a single overriding authoritative reformulating move is missing.

Concluding Comments

It must be admitted that the classroom described here was a low risk environment for the teacher wanting to challenge the rules of conventional classroom interaction, consisting as it did of a small group of students who had chosen to do the *Critical Reading* module. Co-operation could largely be assumed and did not have to be earned through dominative displays of power by the teacher. Nonetheless, it raises questions as to the extent to which we as teachers may miss opportunities for more equitable debate with students across a range of classroom settings. In the *Critical Reading* course there was some evidence that, in however a halting and tentative manner, students were beginning to share in – and in some cases take the initiative in – the construction of and continuing reformulations of text interpretations in a manner which, as argued here, is indicative of classroom based critical literacy. In the case of at least some students it was possible to see evidence not just of an enhanced awareness of textual features but of the ability and willingness to engage in more powerful talk; to draw maximally on shared resources to achieve not definitive but illuminating interpretations of texts. It seems likely that as classroom communities develop over time, teachers can, as Reynolds (1990: 135) puts it, 'use their power in order to share power'. Teachers may be able to loosen the managerial reins allowing both the class participants and themselves to become authors of joint critical enquiry rather than mere animators of classroom discourse.

References

Allwright, D. (1996) Social and pedagogic pressures in the language classroom: The role of socialisation. In H. Coleman (ed.) *Society and the Language Classroom*. Cambridge: Cambridge University Press.

Cassell, P. (ed.) (1993) *The Giddens Reader*. Basingstoke: Macmillan.

Fairclough, N. (1989) *Language and Power*. London: Longman.

Goffman, E. (1981) *Forms of Talk*. Philadelphia: University of Pennsylvania Press.

Habermas, J. (1984) *Theory of Communicative Action, Vol. 1: Reason and the rationalization of society*. Translated by Thomas McCarthy. London: Heinemann.

Hasan, R. (1998) The disempowerment game: Bourdieu and language in literacy Unpublished paper.

Kanpol, B. (1994) *Critical Pedagogy: An introduction*. London: Bergin and Garvey.

Kress, G. (1989) Texture and meaning. In R. Andrews (ed.) *Narrative and Argument*. Milton Keynes: Open University.

Lankshear, C. (1994) *Critical Literacy. Occasional Paper No. 3*. Australian Curriculum Studies Association.

Morgan, W. (1997) *Critical Literacy in the Classroom. The art of the possible*. London and New York: Routledge.

Peled, N. and Blum-Kulka, S. (1998) Dialogue in the Israeli classroom. *Xelkat Lashon 24 Seminar*. Levinsky Publishers.

Pennycook, A. (1994) Incommensurable discourses. *Applied Linguistics* 15 (2), 115–38.

Reynolds, M. (1990) Classroom power – some dynamics of classroom talk. In R. Clark, N. Fairclough, R. Ivanic, N. McLeod, J. Thomas and P. Meara (eds) *Language and Power*. London: Centre for Information on Language Teaching and Research for British Association for Applied Linguistics.

Thomas, J. (1984) Cross-cultural discourse as unequal encounter: Towards a pragmatic analysis. *Applied Linguistics* 5 (3), 226–35.

Wallace, C. (1992) Critical literacy awareness in the EFL classroom. In N. Fairclough (ed.) *Critical Language Awareness.* London: Longman.
Wells, G. (1991) Apprenticeship in literacy. In C. Walsh (ed.) *Literacy as Praxis: Culture, language and pedagogy.* Norwood, NJ: Ablex.
Young, R. (1992) *Critical Theory and Classroom Talk.* Clevedon: Multilingual Matters.

6 Authoring in Student Academic Writing: Regulation and desire

THERESA LILLIS
Sheffield Hallam University

Abstract

This paper is concerned with the tension that student-writers often experience between what they feel they want to say and what they feel they are allowed to say in their academic writing. Whilst signalling the significance of institutional regulation of individual meaning making, I attempt to avoid constructing the student-writers' experience in terms of straightforward dichotomies – between individual and institution, individual and language, regulation and desire – by working with a heuristic based on the work of a number of writers (Bakhtin, 1986; Clark *et al.,* 1990; Fairclough 1992; Ivanic, 1995). The heuristic facilitates an exploration of specific instances of meaning making in academic writing. Examples from two student-writers are discussed in this paper.

Introduction

This paper is an attempt to open up discussion about the ways in which dominant literacy practices within higher education (HE) connect with, and diverge from, individual student-writers' desires for meaning making. The data-experience discussed in the paper – in the form of extracts from student-writers' texts and their talk about these texts – is drawn from a three year research project setting out to explore the experience of a group of 'non-traditional' students and their meaning making in academic writing in HE.[1]

In this paper, I focus on a prominent tension emerging from talk with the student-writers about their texts. At one level, this is a tension between what they feel they want to say and what they feel they are allowed to say in their academic writing, which I am framing here in terms of (individual) desire and (institutional) regulation. However, to construct the student-writers' experience in terms of such a straightforward dichotomy would be to oversimplify the nature of their meaning making, as has recently been signalled by Horner:

> That distinction [between the social and the personal] denies, for example, the possibilities both that 'personal' writing is socially inscribed and that individual students may well have 'personal' interests articulated in more 'academic writing'. (Horner, 1997: 511)

Thus in this paper, whilst acknowledging processes of institutional regulation, I also signal how personal interest, desire, is bound up with dominant ways of meaning in HE.

The paper is organised as follows: firstly, a brief statement about the student-writers whose texts I explore in this paper; secondly, an outline of a heuristic for exploring authoring, based on my understanding of the students' experience in this project and key notions from the work of several writers; thirdly, an exploration of tensions around regulation and desire in specific instances of student authoring, using this heuristic.

The Student Writers in this Paper

Whilst drawing on understandings generated from the research project as a whole, in this paper I focus on specific instances of talk about texts and extracts from written texts of two of the ten student-writers who took part in this project. The examples discussed, whilst few in terms of student numbers, can, I think, be viewed as suggestive of the ways in which desire and regulation are bound up in student academic writing.

The two student-writers whose talk and texts I explore are Nadia and Mary. At the time that we began meeting to discuss their academic writing, Nadia was 20 years old and Mary 21 years old. Both were studying at undergraduate Year 1 level, following a Language Studies course. Nadia is a speaker of Arabic and English, Mary a speaker of Jamaican Creole and English. Both had been through the English state school system to the age of 16.

Exploring Authoring in Student Academic Writing

Why *authoring*?

I am using *authoring* in this paper to signal several things. Firstly, I wish to emphasise the active nature of individual student meaning making. Student-writers make decisions about what and how to write, actively attempting to work out the nature of the conventions relating to the context in which their writing takes place. This often involves inventing/imagining this context. Secondly, viewing student-writers as authors involves an acceptance that writers work with a notion of, as Ivanic says 'the real me', however complex and shifting the nature of this 'real me' (see Ivanic, 1998, chapter 8). It also involves acknowledging that writers work with a notion of 'my own words' relating to this 'real me'. Thirdly, *authoring* is used rather than author in order to signal the dynamic nature of meaning making. These three aspects of authoring are illustrated in the section on students' authoring below.

However, I am not proposing a romantic perspective on student authoring with its inherently transparent view of language (see Reddy, 1979; Wertsch, 1991). But rather, drawing on Bakhtin and Wertsch, I am working with the notion of authoring as the *individual-operating-with-mediational means* (Wertsch, 1991: 96). This involves a rejection of any straightforward dichotomy between individual and language, self and society, and involves working instead with the notion of the individual and language being socioculturally situated in complex ways. By working with the following heuristic when exploring specific instances of authoring, I'm attempting to take into account such complexity.

A heuristic for exploring *authoring*

In exploring specific instances of individual student meaning making, I have found it useful to draw on and connect aspects of the work of several writers. Firstly, Fairclough's three dimensional framework for analysing any discursive event in which he seeks to explicitly explore connections between texts and the contexts of situation and culture (see Halliday, 1978). Within this framework, each event is

> seen as being simultaneously a piece of text, an instance of discursive practice and an instance of social practice. (Fairclough, 1992: 4)

Secondly, I am drawing on and connecting ideas emerging from specific writings by Clark *et al.* (1990) and Ivanic (1995) on authoring in student academic writing. To date, such connections have, I think, remained largely implicit. Here I am suggesting that it is useful to link Clark's three key questions about student meaning making in the institution of HE (see Clark *et al.*, 1990) with Ivanic's three interrelated dimensions of authoring in writing. These dimensions are *authority, authorial presence* and *authorship* (see Ivanic, 1995). Thirdly, I am foregrounding the significance of Bakhtin's notion of *addressivity* for exploring student authoring in HE (see Bakhtin, 1986).

In the diagrams below I outline how the above notions are useful for exploring authoring in student academic writing.

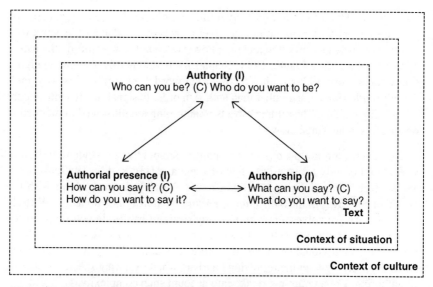

Figure 1 Dimensions to student authoring in academia

After Ivanic, Clark *et al.* (I = Ivanic, 1995; C = Clark *et al.*, 1990) and Fairclough (1992).

I am not suggesting that Clark's questions and Ivanic's dimensions are equivalent in any straightforward way. Ivanic in her writings to date has reserved her three dimensions for referring to the *self as author*, as compared with *the discoursal construction of self* (see Ivanic 1995; see also Clark & Ivanic, 1997); this distinction is not apparent in the work of Clark *et al.* (1990). Moreover, in writings to date, Ivanic's dimensions refer to quite specific aspects of authoring, whereas Clark's terms are significantly broader.[2] However, I find it useful to map the questions/dimensions on to each other in an attempt to construct a heuristic which seeks to avoid a dichotomy between form and content in student authoring. Thus, I have linked Ivanic's notion of *authority* with Clark's question, *who can you be?*, as these both foreground the significance of the writer's feelings of control about the type of person she can be in her academic writing. Who the writer is in her text is, in turn, bound up with what we tend to think of as the content of academic writing and which seems to be encapsulated in Ivanic's notion of *authorship* and Clark's question, *what can you say?* The content, *what you can say*, is both reflected and constituted in the writer's wordings; it is through such wordings – Clark's *how can you say it?* – that the writer's presence – *authorial presence* in Ivanic's terms – comes into being.

Each of these three interconnected dimensions has to be viewed within the contexts of situation and culture. For, as has been argued elsewhere, it is important to acknowledge that when a student sits down to write an essay, even the first time she does so, she is taking part in a particular literacy practice which is bound to a particular social institution The student-writer's meaning making is therefore powerfully mediated by practices at the level of context of situation of the institution, as well as by the ideologically inscribed dominant conventions at the level of context of culture (for literacy practices, see Barton & Hamilton, 1998; Street, 1984, 1995; for discussion of dominant academic literacy practices see Scollon & Scollon, 1981; Gee, 1996; Bizzell, 1992, 1997; Lea & Street, 1998).

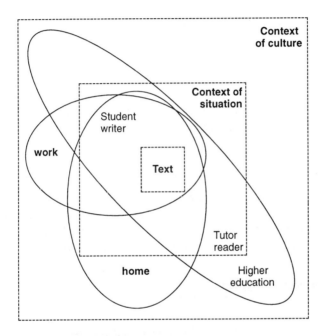

Figure 2 Addressivity and student authoring in Higher Education

The second diagram below points to the importance of Bakhtin's notion of addressivity for exploring connections between specific instances of meaning making and sociodiscursive practices.

Briefly, Bakhtin's notion of *addressivity* refers to the way in which all utterances, spoken and written, involve addressing – directly and/or indirectly – a person, a comment, a question. What is important about addressivity is that the real or imagined addressee contributes to what can be meant as much as the addressor. Thus, individual student meaning making, as indicated by the diagrams, is not only shaped by the voices – as content and wordings – that the student-writer brings to a specific act of writing, but also by the voices that she is attempting to respond to. The most obviously immediate addressee in student writing is the tutor-reader at the level of context of situation. Less obvious, but as significant however, are the voices at the level of context of culture which the student-writer attempts to both draw on and respond to. This dimension of addressivity links with Bartholomae's notion (1985) of student-writers *inventing the university*. Given the denial of real participants within essayist literacy practices, 'invention' rather than negotiation is central to meaning making in student writing and is necessarily a complex activity.[3] In 'inventing' the institutional voices, the student-writers draw on the voices they bring as language and experience from the many sociocultural domains of their lives, as is suggested by the other two spheres in the diagram above which point to home and work.

Bakhtin's notion of addressivity combines with the three dimensions to authoring foregrounded by Clark and Ivanic to provide a useful heuristic for exploring student meaning making, within the contexts of situation and culture of HE. I have this heuristic in mind in the following discussion of specific instances of student meaning making.

Authoring in Student Academic Writing: Focus on regulation

Student-writers do experience direct regulation at the level of context of situation; there are instances of tutors telling student-writers what they cannot say, who they cannot be, how they cannot say it. I have raised this elsewhere (see Lillis, 1997) and here give one example from Nadia's writing.

Table 1 Focus on regulation

Text	Talk about text
I can actually say that I did slip through the system and am unable to identify any support system which has been successfully supporting the bilingualism of minority language speakers, such as myself, during those years.	*This section disappeared in the final draft.* *T asks Nadia why.* N: X *(tutor)* says you shouldn't say that T: Why not? N: He says you don't want to offend anybody. T: So who are you likely to offend? N: The education officers or the education … T: Who's going to read this? N: Just you and X and the moderator. T: So who are you going to offend? N: The education system.

Here Nadia edits out a section of text about her personal experience as a bilingual learner in schools in response to a directive from a tutor. Clearly, what she is not allowed to say in her essay is bound up with who she is not allowed to be; in this instance she is not allowed to draw on her personal experience to be someone who is knowledgeable on educational provision for minority language speakers.

Whilst this is an obvious example of regulation at the level of the context of situation it is important to note that Nadia does not only associate the directive with one individual tutor, but with a more abstract addressee; in this case it is not HE but the *education system*. This more abstract type of addressivity connects with a more common type of regulation that the student-writers experience. This is regulation at the level of context of culture which relates to the dominant culture of HE as well as to British society more generally. Personal desire is not separate from dominant values at the level of context of culture, as is illustrated in the rest of the paper where I focus on tensions around regulation and desire in specific instances of meaning making of two student-writers, Nadia and Mary.

Nadia: *New words bring a little tingle in my ear*

Nadia's overriding concern throughout our discussions was that her own words were *common* and *not good enough* for using in her academic writing. She thus attempted to avoid 'her words' with the result that she often produced confused written text. Consider the examples below.

Table 2 Example 1

Text	Talk about text
When Skinner is trying to identify, that by the gradual bilingual up to on operant behaviour, by reinforcing successive approximation on animals which sustained the response.	*Nadia, talking of the essay in general.* **N:** I've tried to do it to their standard, yeah. **T:** Whose standard? **N:** Well, you know to get a good grade to pass. I've tried to do it, yeah, but I still feel that the assignment isn't good enough. I've tried to change the whole form of writing, like … education … **T:** Actually changing the words that you use? **N:** Yes I've tried changing your everyday like, the way I talk to friends.

Table 3 Example 2

Text	Talk about text
Once this had been repeated several times, the child will instantly know what he or she has done **in order that the adult has said no.** [My emphasis]	*T asks N what the 'in order that …' means.* **N:** I'm quite shocked! I don't know what I've wrote. *T re-reads complete sentence.* **N:** That means that the adult has said no, so the child, cause it's repeated 'no' several times before, the child instantly knows 'no' and knows it's not supposed to do it. *T reads section 'in order that …'* **N:** Because the adult said 'no'. So the child knows that *(hesitant)* **T:** Yeah, go on **N:** So the child knows that it's done wrong because the adult has said so. **T:** Does it made sense now? **N:** Yeah it … I'm quite shocked actually *(laughs)* *T asks where 'in order to' came from* **N:** Because I think I saw it so many times, when it's first written it sounds brilliant! (laughs)

Nadia works at imagining the type of words which will be to *their standard*, 'their' here referring to a non-specific dominant culture of HE as addressee. However, in attempting to use what she imagines to be appropriate language rather than drawing on what she views as her own language, Nadia is often worried that her text will not make sense. The extracts from her written texts above show that her concern is justified. In example 1, although she has clearly attempted to draw on and use lexical items relevant to the specific subject area, she has failed to construct a sentence which is meaningful either for the writer (she couldn't understand what it meant) or for the reader. In example 2, Nadia's talk illustrates how she has avoided using the more obvious (common?) *because* in her attempt to sound more academic and, in so doing, produced confused text.

Thus far, I have emphasised the way in which Nadia feels obliged to avoid her own words and use 'new' words. However, her relationship with new wordings is not (always) negative. On one occasion, talking of 'new' words she states:

They sound good. I don't know (laughs) they bring a little tingle in my ear, yeah. Some words sound really, really nice and I like them.

Nadia here points to a physical enjoyment of new words. She feels excited about using these words as is indicated by her retelling here of an event the previous night.

N: I *(laughs)* used a word on Reba last night.

T: What word was that? It wasn't subtract*

N: No. We were talking about where to meet. I says I'll probably be in Boots. And she says well don't be late because I've got to be at 4 o'clock with Theresa. I says 'I'll take it into consideration' *(laughs)*. She says, 'Nadia, the way you talk' and she starts laughing.

T: So is that a new word, then, consideration?

N: I just made that one up. I just make things up. I don't know, I just pick things and I just use it, words that I like, I'll use them yeah. Reba's noticed it in the lessons as well.

T: What does she say?

N: She says you try and use words in the lessons. I says 'do they sound daft?'. No she says, 'it's as if you're aware of these words, so that's why you're using them'. So I just think oh all right.

*subtractive

This episode reflects the need for an opportunity and space to try out wordings on a real and trustworthy addressee, usually absent in essayist literacy practice, and in so doing trying out not just saying but being somebody else. Following on from her comments above, at a later moment in time, I asked her why she might feel daft about using *take into consideration*:

N: cause I just thought I needed somebody else don't know, I can hear what I'm saying but I can't get the other person's point of view. I asked Reba, yeah, someone close to me, someone I know, who's not going to laugh or say ha ha or take the mick ...

T: Do you think by using those words it sort of changes you?

N: Yeah.

T: How?

N: *(laughs)* I think it puts me up a bit.

T: In what way up a bit?

N: You know, like you've got job prospects, I mean I know I'm only a SUMES *(Sheffield Unified Multicultural Education Service)* staff but I think it puts me the same level as a teacher, a degree level, you know, got a degree and **entitled to use** those words. [My emphasis]

Nadia's physical enjoyment and excitement in using new words is bound up with the opportunity they seem to offer for a change in her social status, as is indicated in her wording *entitled to use those words.* In a more instrumental mode in example 1 (see page 77) she stated that she needs new words to get better marks in her essays. These combined potential benefits resulting from her use of new words stand in contrast to the negative status of her own words which she attempts to avoid. Whilst she clearly enjoys and desires new words, I would suggest that her *subtractive* stance towards the use of her own wordings denies her the possibility of authorial presence and works against Nadia producing meaningful text on many occasions.[4] This adversely affects her chances of success in her courses of study which in turn may prevent her from attaining the social status she desires.

Mary: *I don't want no fancy nonsense. But I do want words*

Mary expresses the view that she wants new words for her meaning making but

> I don't want no fancy nonsense. But I do want words, I do want to improve. Course I do. I *need* it to say what I want to say. Cause what I've got to say needs to be expressed **better**. And I think at the moment, with the vocabulary that I've got, *it's not that bad*. But it doesn't, I miss out a lot of things cause sometimes when you find a better word you can say more things in that one word, whereas when you **go down lower the vocabulary**, it means very few sometimes. You know what I mean? [My emphasis]

Like Nadia, Mary wants new words. But there are significant differences between the two student-writers. Nadia tends to focus on the higher social status she feels the use of new words gives her and takes a subtractive approach towards her own words. Mary too shares Nadia's perspective that particular wordings have a lower status, as is indicated by the wordings in bold in the extract, but in general, Mary takes what seems to be an additive approach to choices about wordings. That is, she says she will use new words **as well** as her words, if she feels they enable her meaning making.

But this meaning making does not take place in a vacuum. Mary's decisions about using particular words are powerfully influenced by how close or distant she feels particular wordings are to her sense of social identity; that is, what she wants to say and how she wants to say (it) are bound up with who she wants to be in HE. Below is an instance of Mary deciding to use a new word – *reinterpreted* – which had emerged during our discussion of a section of her text.

Table 4

Text	Talk about text
	T asks M to explain how she's using Cummins' ideas.
Writing about Black children being sent to schools for the 'educationally subnormal'. Here the interpretation of Cummins' two concepts (CALP and BICS) are anticipated in the opposite direction.	**M:** Well Cummins' concept of surface fluency could be sort of applied to Creolized speech by West Indian children. When any person in education hears them, it gives them the impression, because of the nature of the language and structure, it'll give the impression that this child's incapable of academic work. But sometimes people who speak Creole can read English and understand it quite well. **T:** I think you've got to say something like Cummins' concept of surface fluency has got to be reinterpreted --- **M:** I never knew that such a word existed, 'reinterpreted'. **T:** What other word would you put? **M:** I don't know. I don't think there's anything wrong with it. I think it's all right. I think it saves a lot of, time. Yeah, cause I didn't know what word to use. I was thinking I've got this idea and I can't say it.

Mary uses *reinterpreted* in her final draft. Her decision to use this new word contrasts strongly with her rejection of another word she had briefly considered using in another section of her text: *prerequisite*. She sees this word as *fancy,* as not enabling her meaning making:

> Because prerequisite can be described in a lot of other ways, you see. You don't need it, it's just fancy, it's just an extra word. Reinterpreted, now, which means er being interpreted again in a different way, I can't see any other word for saying that, without having a long string of words and make it unclear.

And she clearly associates *prerequisite* with a social group which has nothing to do with her own:

M: A sort of stereotype I would have would be people who would use words like that are real academics and people sit down and talk about <u>prerequisite</u> *(laughs)* over coffee and tea *(laughs)*. And I just don't experience those kinds of things so why should I … I could be left out from my own community, why am I talking like that for?

T: And you don't want to be part of that community?

M: No, cause I don't fit in cause I'm Black. How can I fit in there? No way, no matter how qualified, how much qualifications, they'll still see me as Black and that's it. And I don't relate to those people anyway, no, no.

Mary says she feels like that about a lot of words. She has particular concerns about how others around her who have not been to college will see her:

> They'll see me differently and I don't want them to, at all. At all. *(laughs)* --- Oh they'll probably say something like erm, what's she using that word to me for? They probably <u>do</u> know what it means but they think there's no need for that. It's unnecessary. It's like putting on airs and graces in a way.

She also has concerns about how she will feel about herself writing in academia:

M: I mean, if I write like that, if I use certain words that are just unnecessary, I'm just going to feel out of it.

T: Out of what? *(They laugh)*

M: Sort of like I'm not me, you know? It's too much of a big stride.

In working at meaning making in her academic writing then in HE, Mary wants words which she feels are part of her existing *habits of meaning* (Halliday, 1978) as well as 'new words' emerging from the context of academia. A prominent criterion Mary works with, in deciding which of the new words she will use, is their potential usefulness. However, this 'usefulness' is bound up with Mary's sense of who she is and wants to be both in relation to her community and the academic institution. Her comments in the extracts above point to a continuum of closeness and distance between particular wordings and Mary's sense of personal/social self. But, as with all the student-writers, she must also work at responding to the context of culture of HE. Thus, although Mary is perhaps the student-writer who most confidently asserts her desire to make decisions about drawing on existing and new habits of meaning, she has also to concern herself with what the abstract addressee of HE will accept. In constructing this addressee, it is important to acknowledge the way in which Mary, and several other student-writers listen out for wordings in a very real sense associated, through individuals, with particular social groups. So Mary says she often looks at sections of her texts and asks herself:

Does that sound right? Have I heard it before? If I have heard it before, who though? Like if my uncle said it, Oh God! *(laughs)*, but if John Major said it last night on TV, it's okay.

In listening out for words that fit, Mary as a Black writer listens specifically for white words – words spoken by powerful white people. And where she can't actually hear such voices, she has to imagine them.

M: Sometimes when I'm writing I think how would they say it? *(laughs)* And I'd like be going through a few sentences before I put it down

T: when you say they

M: [the whites innit?

T: Do you think of all whites speaking the same?

M: Similar

T: You don't think there's a difference in social class?

M: Oh there is there is. But I mean, a <u>particular</u> class <u>obviously</u>, how would they say this?

T: So you had to imagine that then?

M: Yeah. <u>Course</u> I do, I have to imagine it all the time.

T: Are you still doing that now then *(towards middle of her second year in HE)*?

M: Yeah, because it's not me is it?

Thus whilst Mary feels strongly that she wants to take decisions about how her authorial presence – how she says things – connects with the type of authority – who she can be – in her academic texts, her decisions are powerfully influenced by the nature of her imagining of the dominant context of culture.

Conclusion

In this paper I have argued that the tension around regulation and desire is an important dimension to student-writers' authoring in academia.

Working with a heuristic based on the work of Clark and Ivanic on student writing and Bakhtin's notion of addressivity for meaning-making more generally, I have signalled regulation in two ways. Firstly, I have briefly pointed to regulation of student authoring at the level of context of situation; student-writers are sometimes explicitly told to edit out sections of their text. Secondly, I have signalled a more common form of regulation which operates at the level of context of culture. Regulation at this level occurs by students writing with a more abstract type of addressee in mind; this addressee is sometimes named as 'the university' but on many occasions the student-writers work with the notion of 'they', which seems to refer not only to the dominant context of culture of HE but to British society more generally.

Personal desires for meaning making both converge with and diverge from student-writers' understanding of the dominant context of culture of HE. They want to draw on new ways of meaning making from the context of academia, as indicated by their stated desires on many occasions for 'new words'. But they are also aware that new wordings constitute new ways of being, both within their academic texts and their lives, some aspects of which they want to own and others they don't. Whilst there are examples of student-writers including ways of meaning which they desire – for example, Mary's use of some wordings – they often feel profoundly dissatisfied with the type of authoring that seems to be expected. Moreover, there may be major consequences in terms of life chances for individual students. This is the case with Nadia whose rejection of her 'own words' severely affects the possibilities of her success at university and, hence potentially, of the social status she desires.

Appendix: Conventions used for transcribing talk

. , ?	Conventions of punctuation used to indicate in writing my understanding of the sense of the spoken words (see Halliday, 1989: 90)
T	Initial of person speaking
underlining	Word stressed
[	Overlaps/interruptions
...	Long pause (longer than 2 seconds)
(sounds unsure)	Transcriber's comments for additional description
*	Unclear speech
---	Gap in data transcribed

Acknowledgements

Many thanks to all the student-writers who took part in the research project. I am grateful also to Karen Grainger and Roz Ivanic for comments they made on earlier drafts of this paper.

Notes

1. 'Non-traditional' is institutional discourse to refer to students from social groups previously historically excluded from HE. For the research project, see Lillis, 1998.

2. For example, Ivanic to date uses her notion of authorial presence to refer to two aspects of authoring: authoritativeness and the presence of the first person 'I'. See Ivanic, 1995.
3. I have argued elsewhere (see Lillis, 1998) that there is a denial of real participants within essayist literacy practices.
4. I'm using the notions of subtractive/additive from writings on bilingualism. See Lambert, 1977 for use of these terms.

References

Bakhtin, M. M. (1986) The problem of speech genres. In C. Emerson and M. Holquist (eds) *Speech Genres and Other Late Essays.* Translation by V. W. McGee. Austin, Texas: University of Texas Press.

Bartholomae, D. (1985) Inventing the university. In M. Rose (ed.) *When a Writer Can't Write.* New York: Guildford Press.

Barton, D. and Hamilton, M. (1998) *Local Literacies.* London: Routledge.

Bizzell, P. (1992) *Academic Discourse and Critical Consciousness.* Pittsburgh: University of Pittsburgh Press.

Bizzell, P. (1997) Rhetoric and social change. http://www.hu.mtu.edu/cccc/97/bizzell.html.

Clark, R., Cottey, A., Constantinou, C. and Yeoh, O. C. (1990) Rights and obligations in student writing. *Language and Power.* London: Centre for Information on Language Teaching for the British Association for Applied Linguistics.

Clark, R. and Ivanic, R. (1997) *The Politics of Writing.* London: Routledge.

Fairclough, N. (1992) *Discourse and Social Change.* Cambridge: Polity Press.

Gee, J. P. (1996) *Social Linguistics and Literacies. Ideologies in discourses* (2nd edn). Basingstoke: Falmer Press.

Halliday, M. A. K. (1978) *Language as Social Semiotic.* London: Edward Arnold.

Halliday, M. A. K. (1989) *Spoken and Written Language.* Oxford: OUP.

Horner, B. (1997) Students, authorship, and the work of composition. *College English* 59 (5), 505–27.

Ivanic, R. (1995) Writer identity. *Prospect: The Australian Journal of TESOL* 10 (1), 1–31.

Ivanic, R. (1998) *Writing and Identity. The discoursal construction of identity in academic writing.* Amsterdam: Benjamins.

Lambert, W. E. (1977) The effects of bilingualism on the individual: Cognitive, social and socio-cultual consequences. In P. Hornby (ed.) *Bilingualism. Psychological, Social and Educational Implications.* New York: Academic Press.

Lea, M. and Street, B. (1998) Student writing in higher education: an academic literacies approach. *Studies in Higher Education* 23 (2), 157–72.

Lillis, T. (1997) New voices in academia? The regulative nature of academic writing conventions. *Language and Education* 11 (3), 182–99.

Lillis, T. (1998) Making meaning in academic writing: Mature women students in higher education. PhD thesis, Sheffield Hallam University.

Reddy, M. J. (1979) The conduit metaphor: A case of frame conflict in our language about language. In A. Ortony (ed.) *Metaphor and Thought.* Cambridge: CUP.

Scollon, R. and Scollon, S. (1981) *Narrative, Literacy and Face in Interethnic Communication.* Norwood, NJ: Ablex.

Street, B. (1984) *Literacy in Theory and Practice.* London: CUP.

Street, B. (1995) *Social Literacies.* London: Longman.

Wertsch, J. (1991) *Voices of the Mind. A sociocultural approach to mediated action.* London: Harvester Wheatsheaf.

7 Contrastive Rhetoric: New research avenues

ULLA CONNOR
Indiana University in Indianapolis

Abstract

This paper briefly reviews advances in contrastive rhetorical research in second-language writing in the past 30 years but the main focus is on recent applications of contrastive rhetoric in European contexts. The paper suggests how applied linguists might pursue contrastive rhetoric, with varying aims and methods, within different types of institutions such as language departments, departments of international communication, and schools of business. Finally, it discusses the issue of whose norms and standards should be followed.

Introduction

Contrastive rhetoric, according to the Finnish text linguist Enkvist, is 'one of the hot subjects in today's linguistics' (1997: 188). Enkvist continues by asserting that 'contrastive' could be used interchangeably with more familiar words such as 'cross-cultural' or 'intercultural'. Also, 'rhetoric' has a similar connotation with 'text linguistics', 'discourse linguistics', 'discourse analysis', or 'pragmalinguistics'.

Examining the history of contrastive rhetoric, we see that a powerful impetus for its development has come from teachers of foreign languages and second-language composition, especially in the United States. Nevertheless, contrastive rhetoric has potential for other avenues and institutions in the realm of applied linguistics.

In this paper, I will first briefly review the research in contrastive rhetoric in the US applied linguistics context since its birth 30 years ago, giving examples of its most significant contributions. Second, I will discuss how contrastive rhetoric has been pursued and can be pursued with varying aims and methods within different types of institutions in addition to composition studies. Examples will be given from research conducted in Europe. Finally, I will discuss a major issue facing contrastive rhetoric researchers, namely the issue of ideology related to whose norms and standards should be taught in writing.

Contrastive Rhetoric in the US in the Past 30 Years

Contrastive rhetoric has been defined as an area of research in second-language acquisition that identifies problems in composition encountered by second-language writers and, by referring to the rhetorical strategies of the first language, attempts to explain them (Connor, 1996: 5). Initiated 30 years ago in applied linguistics by Robert Kaplan, contrastive rhetoric maintains that language and writing are cultural phenomena. As a consequence each language and culture has rhetorical conventions unique to it. Furthermore, the linguistic and rhetorical conventions of the first language transfer to writing in ESL and often cause interference.

Kaplan's (1966) study was the first serious attempt by US applied linguists to explain the writing of ESL students as opposed to their speaking. Kaplan's pioneering study analysed the organisation of paragraphs in ESL student essays and identified five types of paragraph development, as depicted in the frequently reproduced diagram in Figure 1. It shows how L1 rhetorical structures were evident in the L2 writing of the sample students.

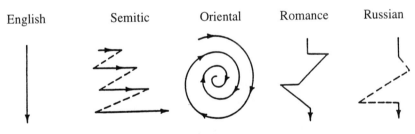

English   Semitic   Oriental   Romance   Russian

Figure 1 Robert Kaplan's diagram of five patterns of paragraph organisation (1966: 257)

As is well-known, Kaplan's contrastive rhetoric has been criticised for several reasons: being too ethnocentric and privileging the writing of native English speakers as well as ignoring linguistic and cultural differences in writing among different languages, e.g. Chinese, Thai, and Korean speakers in one Oriental group. Kaplan himself has modified his earlier position, leaning away from what could be described as Whorfian interpretation, namely that rhetorical patterns reflect patterns of thinking in L1. Instead, cross-cultural differences in writing can be explained by different conventions of writing, which are learned, rather than acquired.

Kaplan's model, being concerned with paragraph organisation, was useful in explaining essays written by college students for academic purposes. However, it was not particularly useful in describing writing for academic and professional purposes. Neither was it useful in describing composing processes across cultures.

To expand Kaplan's original work, significant changes have taken place in contrastive rhetoric in the past 30 years. In a book published in 1996, I survey the field and suggest that contrastive rhetoric has taken new directions in the following four domains:

(1) Contrastive textlinguistics
These studies examine, compare, and contrast how texts are formed and interpreted in different languages and cultures using methods of written discourse analysis. See Clyne, 1987; Connor & Kaplan, 1987; Eggington, 1987; Hinds, 1983, 1987, 1990.

(2) The study of writing as a cultural and educational activity
These studies investigate literacy development in L1 language and culture and examine effects on the development of L2 literacy. See Carson, 1992; Purves, 1988.

(3) Classroom based studies of writing
These examine cross-cultural patterns in process writing, collaborative revisions, and student-teacher conferences. See Allaei & Connor, 1990; Goldstein & Conrad, 1990; Hull, Rose, Fraser & Castellano, 1991; Nelson & Murphy, 1992.

(4) Contrastive genre-specific studies
These examine a variety of genres in academic and professional writing, e.g. journal articles, business reports, letters of application, grant proposals, editorials, etc. See Bhatia, 1993; Connor, Davis, & De Rycker, 1995; Jenkins & Hinds, 1987; Mauranen, 1993; Swales, 1990; Tirkkonen-Condit, 1996; Ventola & Mauranen, 1991.

An example from each category illustrates the focus of each domain. In text linguistic studies in the 1980s, perhaps the work with most impact was that of the late John Hinds, who compared patterns of coherence across Japanese texts and texts in English. Hinds found that many newspaper columns in Japan followed the ancient organisational pattern of ki-shoo-ten-ketsu, or begin your argument, develop it, turn to material with a connection but not direct association with the text, and conclude. In reading direct translations of Japanese writing in various genres, native English speakers found the introduction of the 'ten' section incoherent. Based on his work, Hinds suggested that Japanese writing is more reader responsible than English writing. In numerous publications, Hinds also argued that native English speakers prefer a deductive type of argument. Although they are familiar with induction, they are not used to reading prose organised in ways other than induction and deduction.

Among studies investigating academic literacy development in L1 language and culture, the most comprehensive research was conducted by Purves (1988) and others in the IEA research group. Fourteen countries were included in the ambitious international study of writing achievement. The research yielded significant findings about the writing patterns of students at three age levels – 12,16, and 18, writing for three different purposes: narration, exposition, and argumentation. One major contribution was the increased understanding about the importance of the tertium comparationis, or the common platform of comparison. For example, expectations about what an argumentative essay entails vary from culture to culture; in some cultures a good argumentative essay is a story.

Classroom studies have been conducted to study patterns of collaboration in writing groups in writing classes. The research of Carson (1992) and Nelson & Murphy (1992) at Georgia State University is the most extensive; through text analyses and transcripts of collaborative writing sessions, they have found, among other things, that Chinese speaking ESL writers are more concerned about harmony than correction in the writing groups, while Spanish speaking students in the groups consider their roles to be that of critics. Implications for multi-cultural writing groups in the US are obvious.

Genre specific contrastive studies have extended the contrastive framework well beyond student writing. Tirkkonen-Condit (1996), for example, has contrasted the discourse of newspaper editorials in Finland, England, and the US, and has found, using various textual analyses, that editorials in Finnish newspapers are typically written to build consensus while in the US they argue for a particular point of view.

What has been learned about writing across cultures in these 30 years of contrastive rhetoric research? It has been found that all cultural groups engage in a variety of types of writing, each with their own conventional preferences and tendencies. It has also been found that what constitutes straightforward writing depends on the reader. Thus, Kaplan's diagram of the linear line of argument by native English speakers may accurately represent the perception of native English speakers but not necessarily that of speakers of other languages. At a TESOL colloquium in honour of Kaplan's work in 1996, I proposed new diagrams. The playfully drawn 'squiggles' shown in Figures 2–4 show that the writing of native English speakers, such as article introductions, does not follow a linear pattern. Neither does the development of letters of job application by US writers appear linear while the writing by Belgians does (see Connor *et al.*, 1995a). Finally, the research by Ventola & Mauranen (1991) and Mauranen (1993) suggests that the writing of Finns, in Finnish and English, follows a circular pattern of organisation.

Figure 2 New diagrams

English Article Introductions

(Swales, 1990)

(1) Establish territory

(2) Summarise previous research

(3) Indicate a gap

(4) Introduce present research

Figure 3

'Moves' in Letter of Job Application

US	*Belgian*	*Asian*
Apply for position	Apply for position	Apply for position
Include résumé	Include résumé	Include résumé
Explain qualifications		Ask for pity
Express desire for interview		Express apology
Explain how to be reached		
Express pleasantries		

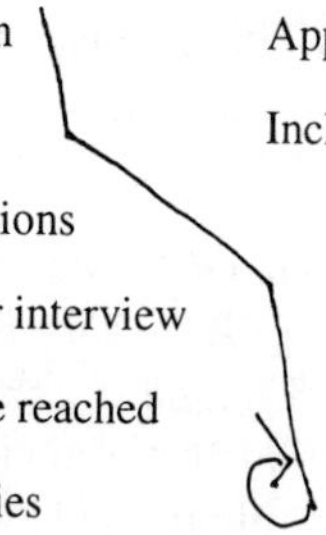

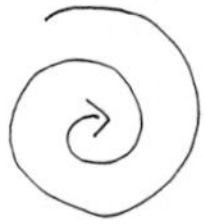

Figure 3

Finnish expository paragraph

(Mauranen, 1993)

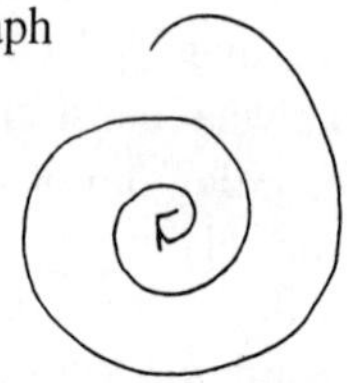

These playfully drawn diagrams are meant to show that coherence lies in the eye of the beholder and that one needs to exercise care in attaching labels to others' writing.

Applications of Contrastive Rhetoric in Europe

Enkvist, in his 1997 article 'Why we need contrastive rhetoric' suggests that contrastive rhetoric could be pursued with varying aims and methods within different institutions at universities and outside. He shows how contrastive rhetoric is of interest to many units catering for training in foreign language skills at universities in Finland. First, universities have language departments, which teach language, literature, linguistic and literary theory and applied linguistics. Secondly, for the past 25 years, Finland has had language centres at universities teaching languages for specific purposes and providing translation and editing services. The third type of language teaching establishment in Finland with potential for contrastive rhetoric is the School of International Communication. A fourth type of institution interested in contrastive rhetoric is the School of Economics. Figure 5 is a diagram created by Enkvist to show the applications of contrastic rhetoric in Europe.

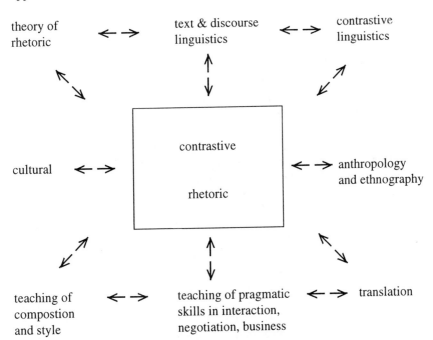

Figure 5 Applications of contrastive rhetoric in Europe (Enkvist, 1997)

The following examples illustrate the use of the contrastive rhetoric framework in research relevant to academic and professional settings in Europe, including institutions mentioned by Enkvist.

Academic writing
(in Language Departments and Language Centres)

Research on academic writing conducted in the contrastive framework focuses on two genres: research articles and grant proposals. The work of Ventola & Mauranen (1991) in Finland has shown convincingly the value of text analyses in a contrastive framework. Their research relates to cultural differences between Finnish and English-speaking research writers. Their contrastive text linguistic project investigated language revision practices by native English speakers in Finnish scientists' articles written in English and also compared those texts to articles by native English speaking writers. A contrastive systemic linguistic study found that Finnish writers used connectors less frequently and in a less varied fashion than native writers. In reference use, the Finnish writers tended to use the article system inappropriately, and there were also differences in thematic progression. Other research by Mauranen (1993) found that, in addition, native English speakers used more text about text, or metatext, and also preferred placing the statement of their main point later in the text than native English speakers.

In a project, playfully titled 'Milking Brussels', in which we analysed research grant proposals written by Finnish scientists for the European Union research funds, it was discovered that Finnish writers had these same difficulties when writing grant proposals – such as not stating their theses at the beginning of the writing but preferring to delay the introduction of the purpose (Connor *et al.*, 1995b). Other textual differences in the Finnish writers' proposals included a lack of transitions and other metatext to guide the reader, differences similar to the ones found in Ventola's and Mauranen's research on academic research articles discussed above.

In addition to non-genre specific textual features such as the use of transitions or placement of main ideas in text, differences were found at the genre-specific level. In sections about the aims of research, the Finns would not make as strong statements about the goals and deliverables. Instead, they state that the system 'will aim for the following capabilities: (1) estimate the numerical value of key materials properties such as … (2) detect the presence of structurally significant localised defects such as …' The British researchers, on the other hand, tended to begin their paragraphs with a strong statement of goals using active sentences with the goals as the sentence subject.

Table 1 Sample goal statements from two European Union grant proposals

---

Excerpt from Finnish proposal

---

1. The deliverables in this project are:

   The research project will develop a system for the non-destructive inspection and evaluation of monolithic refractory products. The system developed will aim for the following target capabilities: (1) estimate the numerical value of key material properties such as ... (2) detect the presence of structurally significant localised defects such as ...

Excerpt from British proposal

---

2. The long-term goal of this proposal is to develop an approach to a post mass-production paradigm. This is a paradigm which recognises the imbalances caused by the present global manufacturing environment ... To support this long-term goal, this test case aims to develop systematisation of knowledge for design and manufacturing and the concept of the virtual factory ... The concept of virtual factory to generate dynamic product-specific product-lines for configurable products with functional knowledge will be developed and demonstrated.

   The object of this study is to establish a harmonised test method and standards for measuring slip resistance of protective footwear on the basis of existing methodology and test rigs. In trying to achieve this object, the focus will be on bridging the gap between mechanical test methods and test methods involving human subjects by in detail analysing mechanical circumstances in human subjects and translating them into mechanical tests.

Another crosscultural difference in the EU proposals comes from the personnel section of the proposals, in which the competence of the researchers is highlighted. The first example is a short biographical statement written by a Finnish scientist. The scientist lists his/her academic appointments as well as the numbers of theses and dissertations supervised and papers published. No evaluation of the background and experience relative to the project is apparent, as shown in Table 2.

In contrast, the second illustration in Table 2 is a biography of a Swedish researcher. The statement is not a mere list; instead, two strong positive appraisals are included: 'a very distinguished academic record' and 'the department has excellent facilities'.

Table 2 Sample competence claims in European Union grant proposals

---

1. Prof. N.N. joined the Department of ... in 19xx. He has been involved in X
    in Finland and abroad since 19xx. During 19xx–19xx he acted as the head of
    ... On joining U University, N.N. initiated a research and teaching program
    focused mainly on the effects of E on the quality of Y. He has recently been
    appointed Assisting Co-leader of the UNESCO-sponsored project, which is
    aimed at ... At present two PhD theses and five MSc thesis projects are
    being carried out. A number of abstracts have been published, some of
    which are mentioned in the list of publications below and the manuscripts of
    some of these are being in different stages of preparation for publication in
    international journals.

---

2. Professor N.N. has a very distinguished academic record with over 150
    publications in scientific journals, books, and conference proceedings
    since 19xx including 80 publications in the last eight years. He has made
    over 65 presentations (oral and posters) at international meetings and
    over 20 at national scientific symposia, conferences and workshops, includ-
    ing several invited and plenary lectures since 19xx. He has led over 20
    research grants and contracts as principal investigator and is a member
    of over 12 boards and scientific and technical committees. He has also
    undertaken consulting activities in relation to industrial problems of P.
    His teaching activities include courses in chemistry, processes in P and
    population control since 19xx. He has supervised 20 graduate students
    (PhD) since 19xx. The Department has excellent facilities for experimental
    studies of environmental systems, presently focused on ... 25 theses have
    been submitted in the last x years. Additional members of the proposer's
    team will include Dr A.A., Professor B.B., Dr C.C. and Polish and German
    Contacts.

My sense of different rhetorical patterns between American English and
Finnish was reinforced while we were producing a guide to writing grants in
English for Finnish grant applicants. The book was based on the team's research
and the process of writing as a team was an experience in contrastive rhetoric.
The guidebook set out to describe how English writing differs from Finnish
therefore it was important to state right at the start the purpose of the book and
how important it is for Finns to learn to state their main points at the beginning,
give examples, and provide transitions throughout the text and repeat the main
point. The Finnish research assistant in the team wrote the first draft, which I

found incoherent. I made suggestions in the margins such as 'we need to state the main point at the beginning of the paragraph', and 'we shouldn't jump around with ideas, and leave the most important thing as the very last in the book'. My summary comments on the draft to the RA and the team read (translated from Finnish):

> Perhaps I'm reading this text as an American. It's all fine text but I find it incoherent in places, hard to follow. I expect the main point at the beginning of the paragraph. I expect a paragraph to contain examples about the main point – no jumping between several points. If others [the other researchers in the project] don't object to the current presentation, I must be completely Americanised.

Business and other professional writing

With the globalisation of business and other professional communication, writing in such professional genres as letters, résumés, and job applications for readers with a different language and cultural background than one's own is a reality for more and more people. It has been found that in these contexts, too, second language writers transfer patterns and styles from the first language to the second. Predictably, differing reader expectations cause misunderstandings. For example, requests in letters can be made too directly when directness is more esteemed in the first language than in the second. Résumés also differ in style cross-culturally and even intraculturally, as in the difference between the functional résumé and traditional résumé in the United States. A special issue of *Multilingua: Journal of Cross-cultural and Interlanguage Communication* (1996, 15, 3) included three papers dealing with contrastive research of professional writing in Europe. A summary of the studies follows.

Tirkkonen-Condit (1996) compared Finnish and Anglo-American argumentation in editorials and found that Finns argue more implicitly than do American and British writers. Finns do not use explicit arguments because the society values consensus and because the culture is highly context dependent and relies more on the status of the writer than on his/her evidence.

Upon the examination of politeness strategies in business letters, Yli-Jokipii (1996) suggests that Finnish letters show deferential politeness and tend to refrain from exercising social power. Yli-Jokipii shows ways in which Finnish writers signal 'politeness' such as the avoidance of expressing human agents and using the impersonal passive instead.

Fredrickson (1996) provides a multi-level analysis of court documents in Sweden and the US The data came from 24 court cases; for each case the documents studied were the brief of the appellant, the brief of the appellee, and the opinion of the Appeals Court. The results show complex relationships among genres and ethnic cultures. Cultural differences are apparent at all the levels of analysis. However, Fredrickson points out many of the differences are explained by the institutional conventions and expectations in the two legal cultures. For example, American briefs are much longer than Swedish briefs because briefs in the American court are extremely important, as the legal system depends heavily on precedents. It is clear then that contrastive rhetoric study is now proving of use beyond the academic world.

Whose Norms and Standards?

A major question in contrastive rhetoric deals with an ideological problem about whose norms and standards to teach and the danger of perpetuating established power roles. This has been raised as an issue in postmodern discussion about discourse and the teaching of writing (Kubota, 1999; Ramanathan & Atkinson, 1999). The discussion has, of course, been at the forefront of contrastive rhetoric studies; recent critics of contrastive rhetoric have criticised contrastive rhetoricians for teaching L2 students to write for L1 native speaker expectations instead of allowing them to express their own native language and culture identities. Researchers working in the contrastive rhetoric paradigm have maintained that cultural differences to acculturate EFL writers to the target discourse community need to be explicitly taught. They maintain that teachers of English or consultants in grant proposal writing need to teach students or clients about the expectations of their readers. Thus, at workshops for Finnish scientists about how to write proposals in English, we taught a Western, generic style of grant proposal writing using a set of moves we had developed. We instructed the Finnish scientists that if they wished to get EU research grants, they needed to follow the EU norms and expectations, which, three years ago, at least, were based on Anglo-American scientific and promotional discourse. When, on the other hand, Finnish scientists write grant applications in Finnish, they should follow the expectations of the Finnish agencies. Although the decision about language choice seems more straightforward in the case of grant proposals in the project described above, it may be more complex in the case of student writers in undergraduate colleges in the US. Postmodern theories encouraging the preservation of the native language and style may be more appropriate for preserving the national identity of immigrant students for example. This is not such an issue in the case of professional and academic writing.

In the EU project proposal, however, we became aware of another issue facing contrastive rhetoric, namely that soon there may not be an English-language norm for the writing of EU grant proposals. It seems clear that there may be changes in the norms, and standards of English in grant proposals because the raters of grant proposals for the EU in Brussels are not only native speakers of English but are scientists from all EU countries with many different first languages and many different rhetorical orientations. In fact, something called Eurorhetoric has probably emerged. This blurring of standards and norms in written language is consistent with recent developments in spoken language. David Crystal (1997), for example, suggests that a new kind of English, World Standard Spoken English (WSSE) may be emerging for use in situations where there is a need to communicate in English with people from other countries for purposes of business, industry, and diplomacy. Little, however, has yet been conjectured about the nature of this world English, and no theoretical model, as is the case with Eurorhetoric, has been established.

Recent discussions suggesting that it is not possible to draw rigid boundaries between cultures have affected research directions in contrastive rhetoric. Modern contrastive rhetoric does not treat writing in different cultures as monolithic and static but is aware of the differences that genres and situations impose on writing, as I hope this review of contrastic rhetoric in academic and professional genres has shown.

References

Allaei, S. K. and Connor, U. M. (1990) Exploring the dynamics of cross-cultural collaboration in writing classrooms. *The Writing Instructor* 10 (1), 19–28.

Bhatia, V. K. (1993) *Analyzing genre: Language use in professional settings.* New York: Longman.

Carson, J. G. (1992) Becoming biliterate: First language influences. *Journal of Second Language Writing* 1 (1), 37–60.

Charles, M. (1996) Business negotiations: Interdependence between discourse and the business relationship. *English for Specific Purposes* 15 (1), 19-36.

Clyne, M. (1987) Cultural differences in the organization of academic texts: English and German. *Journal of Pragmatics* 11 (2), 211–47.

Connor, U. (1996) *Contrastive Rhetoric: Cross-cultural aspects of second language writing.* New York: Cambridge University Press.

Connor, U. and Kaplan, R. B. (eds) (1987) *Writing Across Languages: Analysis of L2 text.* Reading, MA: Addison-Wesley.

Connor, U., Davis, K. and DeRycker, T. (1995a) Correctness and clarity in applying for overseas jobs: A cross-cultural analysis of US and Flemish applications. *Text* 15 (4), 457–75.

Connor, U., Helle, T., Mauranen, A., Ringbom, H., Tirkkonen-Condit, S. and Yli-Antola, M. (1995b) *Tehokkaita Eu-projecktiehdotuksia. Ohjeita kirjoittajile (Successful strategies for writers of EU grant proposals).* Helsinki, Finland: TEKES.

Connor, U. and Mauranen, A. (in press). Grant proposals: A model for analysis. *English for Specific Purposes Journal.*

Crystal, D. (1997) *English as a Global Language.* Cambridge: Cambridge University Press.

Eggington, W. (1987) Written academic discourse in Korean: Implications for effective communication. In U. Connor and R. B. Kaplan (eds) *Writing Across languages: Analysis of L2 text* (pp. 153–68). Reading, MA: Addison-Wesley.

100   LANGUAGE AND LITERACIES

Enkvist, N. E. (1997). Why we need contrastive rhetoric. *Alternation* 4 (1), 188–206.
Fredrickson, K. (1996) Contrasting genre systems: Court documents from the United States and Sweden. *Multilingua* 15 (3), 275–304.
Goldstein, L. M. and Conrad, S. M. (1990) Student input and negotiation of meaning in ESL writing conferences. *TESOL Quarterly* 24 (3), 443–60.
Hinds, J. (1983) Contrastive rhetoric: Japanese and English. *Text* 3 (2), 183–95.
Hinds, J. (1987) Reader versus writer responsibility: A new typology. In U. Connor and R. B. Kaplan (eds) *Writing Across Languages: Analysis of L2 text* (pp. 141–52). Reading, MA: Addison-Wesley.
Hinds, J. (1990). Inductive, deductive, quasi-inductive: Expository writing in Japanese, Korean, Chinese, and Thai. In U. Connor and A. M. Johns (eds) *Coherence: Research and pedagogical perspectives* (pp. 87–110). Arlington, VA: TESOL.
Hull, G. Rose, M., Fraser, K. L., and Castellano, M. (1990) Remediation as a social construct: Perspectives from an analysis of classroom discourse. *College Composition and Communication* 42 (3), 299–329.
Jenkins, S. and Hinds, J. (1987) Business letter writing: English, French and Japanese. *TESOL Quarterly* 21 (2), 327–50.
Kaplan, R. B. (1966) Cultural thought patterns in intercultural education. *Language Learning* 16 (1), 1–20.
Kubota, R. (1999) Japanese culture constricted by discourses: Implications for applied linguistics research and ELT. *TESOL Quarterly* 33 (1), 9–36.
Mauranen, A. (1993) *Cultural Differences in Academic Rhetoric.* Fankfurt am Main: Peter Lang.
Nelson, G. L. and Murphy, J. M. (1992) An ESL writing group: Task and social dimensions. *Journal of Second Language Writing* 1 (3), 171–94.
Purves, A. C. (1988) *Writing Across Languages and Cultures: Issues in contrastive rhetoric.* Newbury Park, CA: Sage.
Ramanathan, V. and Atkinson, D. (1999) Individualism, academic writing, and ESL writers. *Journal of Second Language Writing* 8 (1), 45–75.
Swales, J. M. (1990) *Genre Analysis. English in academic and research settings.* New York: Cambridge University Press.
Tirkkonen-Condit, S. (1996) Explicitness vs. implicitness of argumentation: An intercultural comparison. *Multilingua* 15 (3), 257–74.
Ventola, E. and Mauranen, A. (1991) Non-native writing and native revising of scientific articles. In E. Ventola (ed.) *Functional and Systemic Linguistics* (pp. 457–92). Berlin: Mouton De Gruyter.
Ventola, E. and Mauranen, A. (1996) (eds) *Academic Writing: Intercultural and textual issues.* Amsterdam: Benjamins.
Yli-Jokipii, H. (1996) An approach to contrasting languages and cultures in the corporate context: Finnish, British, and American business letters and telefax messages. *Multilingua* 15 (3), 305–28.

8 The 1998 Reform of German Orthography

SALLY JOHNSON
University of Lancaster

Abstract

In November 1995, after many years of debate by linguists and politicians, it was announced that a reform of German orthography would be officially introduced from 1998. No sooner had the reform been agreed, however, than widespread public protest began, such that by 1996 the issue of how the German language should be written had evolved into a major political wrangle, requiring intervention on the part of the Federal Constitutional Court.

In spite of frequent media discussion during the past few years, the dispute over German orthographic reform has, for many observers, remained somewhat perplexing, touching as it does, not only on principles of linguistics, but also the finer points of German constitutional law. The aim of this paper is therefore to describe and analyse that dispute, before locating it within the theoretical framework of language standardisation and the so-called 'complaint tradition', described by Milroy & Milroy (1999).

Introduction

On 30 November 1995, a press release by the Standing Conference of the Ministers of Education and the Arts of the 16 Federal German States (*Kultusministerkonferenz* – KMK) announced that a reform of German orthography had been approved. Known in German as the *Rechtschreibreform*, the proposed changes were an attempt to simplify what was perceived by many to be a complex and inconsistent set of orthographic rules, causing unnecessary problems for language users of all ages, but in particular for young school-children. The reform was to be implemented from 1 August 1998 to coincide with the start of the new school year. There would then be a seven-year transition period until 2005, during which the old orthography would be considered 'dated' (*überholt*) but not 'wrong' (*falsch*). However, many Federal states or *Bundesländer* chose not to delay implementation until 1998, instructing schools in their area to begin teaching the new rules from the start of the school year 1996/7.

The decision to reform German orthography was not taken lightly – nor was it an exclusively German affair. The final proposal was the result of many years of often heated debate amongst educationalists, linguists, politicians and other interested parties from the Federal Republic of Germany, Austria, and Switzerland, as well as German-speaking groups in Belgium, Denmark, Italy, Liechtenstein, Luxembourg, Romania, and Hungary. On 1 July 1996, representatives from these countries met in Vienna in order to ratify the reform via the so-called 'Viennese Declaration of Intent' (*Wiener Absichtserklärung*). Significantly, no parliamentary law (*Gesetz*) was anticipated by any of those involved. Instead, the reform was to be introduced via decree (*Erlass*), which, in the case of Germany, was to be ordained via the individual education ministers of the 16 Federal states.

Since the summer of 1996, however, the reform has been the focus of significant public and media controversy. Indeed, at various times between 1996 and 1998, it was not always clear whether the proposed changes were even constitutionally viable. Though the reform did ultimately go ahead as planned on 1 August 1998, there are still a number of questions which remain unresolved. The aim of this paper is therefore two-fold. In the first section, I shall outline the structural amendments made to German orthography, and consider some of the linguistic issues these have raised. In the second section, I shall describe the constitutional challenge to which the reform has been subject in Germany (though leaving aside the question of Austria and Switzerland), before going on to explore the theoretical implications of that dispute from a sociolinguistic point of view.

Details of the Reform

The last reform of German orthography took place in 1901/2, though this in itself was not undisputed (see Sauer & Glück, 1995). Moreover, one of its main authors, Konrad Duden, declared the reform to be little more than an intermediate step on the path towards further revisions (Russ, 1994: 165). Since that time, virtually every year has seen a failed attempt to achieve the kinds of revisions to which Duden had referred (see Jansen-Tang, 1988; Küppers, 1984; Scheuringer, 1996).

The version of the reform which was finally agreed for 1998 affects six main aspects of German orthography. The following is a brief summary of the proposed changes and some of the linguistic issues they raised (for more precise details, see *Deutsche Rechtschreibung*, 1996; Heller, 1997).

(1) Sound/letter relationships (*Laut-Buchstaben-Zuordnung*)

Alterations to sound/letter (or phoneme/grapheme) relationships affect three main areas of German orthography. First, there has been an attempt to harmonise spellings in a way which will highlight the morphological relationship between word groups:

OLD SPELLING	NEW SPELLING	ENGLISH
behende	behände (*like:* Hand)	nimble
belemmert	belämmert (*like:* Lamm)	awful
Stengel	Stängel (*like:* Stange)	stem
numerieren	nummerieren (*like:* Nummer)	to number
Ballettänzer	Balletttänzer (*like:* Ballett+tänzer)	ballet dancer
Tolpatsch	Tollpatsch (*like:* toll)	clumsycreature
rauh	rau (*like:* grau, schlau)	rough
substantiell	substanziell (*like:* Substanz)	substantial
Känguruh	Känguru (*like:* Gnu)	kangaroo

A particular source of media derision has been the change which now permits three consecutive graphemes, as in the compounds *Balletttänzer* (ballet dancer) or *Seeelefant* (sea elephant), even though the option of hyphenation, e.g. *Ballett-Tänzer* or *See-Elefant*, constitutes an official alternative (see Scheuringer, 1996: 118).

Second, the use of the graphemes <ss> and <ß> has been regulated. For example, <ss> is now to be written after short vowels:

OLD SPELLING	NEW SPELLING	ENGLISH
küssen/Kuß	küssen/Kuss	to kiss/kiss
lassen/läßt	lassen/lässt	to leave/leaves
daß	dass	that

but <ß> retained after long vowels such as *Maß* (measure) or *Straße* (street), and following diphthongs such as *draußen* (outside) and *beißen* (to bite).

This rule has been the focus of criticism from opponents, as well as those broadly in favour of the reform who would nonetheless have advocated a more radical change. On the one hand, both groups have argued that the shift from *daß→dass* fails to eliminate the source of many errors amongst young learners, namely the inability to distinguish between the subordinating conjunction *dass* (that/which) and the relative pronoun *das* (that/which). On the other hand, the new rule scarcely constitutes a *simplification* of spelling given that it requires users to differentiate (phonetically) between various types of vowel sounds (Denk, 1997; Poschenrieder, 1997). Having said this, the reformers themselves are at pains to point out that the total replacement of <ß> with <ss> (in line with Swiss usage) was never on the *political* agenda (Augst & Schaeder, 1997: 15).

Finally, the spelling of loan words, a continual stumbling block over the years, could not be resolved one way or the other. It was therefore agreed to allow equal validity to both the original and the germanicised variant – itself an ongoing source of controversy (ibid: 20–1):

OLD SPELLING	NEW SPELLING	ENGLISH
Diskothek	Diskotek/Diskothek	discotheque
Geographie	Geografie/Geographie	geography
Joghurt	Jogurt/Joghurt	yog(h)urt
Spaghetti	Spagetti/Spaghetti	spaghetti
Chicorée	Schikoree/Chicorée	chicory
Ketchup	Ketschup/Ketchup	ketchup
Thunfisch	Tunfisch/Thunfisch	tuna
Portemonnaie	Portmonee/Portemonnaie	purse

One of the opponents' concerns here is that such legitimised variation might generate a social and political stratification of spelling. Denk, for example, fears that one form may come to be viewed as the 'educated' variant, thus revealing the *lack* of erudition on the part of those who choose the other (1997: 42–3). For Gröschner and Kopke, on the other hand, the concern is that the use of the older variant might 'out' the user as 'conservative' in the wider sense (1997: 299).

(2) Writing lexical items as one word or two
(Getrennt- und Zusammenschreibung – GZS)

This has been one of the most problematical areas of German orthography, and one left untouched by the original 1901/2 regulations. After years of deliberation, the 1998 reform finally stipulated that the following items should be written separately:

OLD SPELLING	NEW SPELLING	ENGLISH
radfahren	Rad fahren (*like:* Auto fahren)	to ride a bicycle
sitzenbleiben	sitzen bleiben	to repeat a school year
übrigbleiben	übrig bleiben (*like:* artig grüßen)	to be left over
soviel	so viel (*like:* so viele)	as much
wieviel	wie viel (*like:* wie viele)	how much

whereas the following should be written together:

OLD SPELLING	NEW SPELLING	ENGLISH
irgend etwas	irgendetwas	anything/something
irgend jemand	irgendjemand	anyone/someone

The main objection here relates to what opponents see as the 'privileging' of orthography over meaning (Denk, 1997: 42–3). For example, according to the old rules, the infinitive *sitzenbleiben* (to repeat a school year) could be differentiated from its counterpart *sitzen bleiben* (to remain seated). In this regard, the new spelling arguably constitutes an impoverishment of the lexicon. But frequently overlooked by critics is the fact that such semantic distinctions are routinely forfeited in finite verb constructions such as the first person *ich bleibe sitzen*, which can never mark the semantic difference in the same way as the infinitives. As in most other cases, the actual meaning is then clarified by the context of usage, e.g. whether I intend to 'remain seated' or am required to 'repeat a year at school' (see Augst & Schaeder, 1997: 22–35).

(3) Hyphenation *(Schreibung mit Bindestrich)*

The following changes have been made with regard to the use of hyphens:

OLD SPELLING	NEW SPELLING	ENGLISH
Hair-Stylist	Hairstylist/Hair-Stylist	—
Job-sharing	Jobsharing/Job-Sharing	—
Shopping-Center	Shoppingcenter/Shopping-Center	—
17jährig	17-jährig	17 year-old
100prozentig	100-prozentig	100 per cent
Ballettruppe	Balletttruppe/Ballett-Truppe	ballet troupe

This has probably been one of the least controversial areas of the reform, though objections have been raised regarding the use of hyphens in foreign (especially English) loans. For example, Denk (1997: 44) highlights the irony that pupils will now learn one set of spellings in their German lessons (e.g. *Centrecourt/Centre-Court*), but will be taught the 'correct' spelling (centre court) in their English classes.

(4) The use of upper- and lower-case letters *(Groß- und Kleinschreibung – GKS)*

Even today, German remains the only world language to insist on the capitalisation of *all* nouns. This is a feature of German orthography which has traditionally caused problems for some people, not least due to the many inconsistencies in usage, which have arisen over the years. However, reactions to earlier reform proposals signalled that the abolition of noun capitalisation and the adoption of usage more akin to English (known as 'moderate minisculisation' or *gemäßigte Kleinschreibung*) was unlikely to meet with popular approval. It was in this context that reformers opted for the least controversial alternative of harmonising the existing rules (see Scheuringer, 1996: 125):

OLD SPELLING	NEW SPELLING	ENGLISH
in bezug auf	in Bezug auf	with respect to
(*but:* mit Bezug auf)		
radfahren	Rad fahren	to cycle
(*but:* Auto fahren)		
der/die/das letzte	der/die/das Letzte	the last one
im großen und ganzen	im Großen und Ganzen	on the whole
gestern abend	gestern Abend	yesterday evening
am Sonntag abend	am Sonntagabend	on Sunday evening
Sonntag abends	sonntagabends	on Sunday evenings
auf deutsch	auf Deutsch	in German

By contrast, the use of capital letters in certain forms of address has been abolished. For example, lower-case characters are now to be used in the familiar forms of the second person, both in the singular – *du* (you), *dein* (your), *dich/dir* (to you) – and plural – *ihr* (you), *euer* (your), *euch* (to you). This compares to the previous tradition of writing *Du* and *Ihr*, etc. with capital letters, although the polite forms *Sie* (you) and *Ihr* (your) continue to be capitalised.

Again, these proposals have been widely criticised. Opponents claim, for example, that the distinction between the new spellings in such phrases as *morgen <u>Abend</u>* (tomorrow evening) and *morgen <u>früh</u>* (tomorrow morning – literally 'tomorrow early') will be difficult to apply in practice. In many ways this is true. However, as Augst and Schaeder (1997: 36) point out, such changes are the logical outcome of the decision to harmonise existing rules, given that the abolition of noun capitalisation was rejected as a workable option. This is because the adaptation of the old spellings *morgen abend* and *morgen früh* results in the capitalisation of nouns such as *Abend* (evening), but not other word classes such as the adverb *früh* (early).

(5) Punctuation (Zeichensetzung)

Punctuation was a further area not dealt with by the 1901/2 reform, though a number of rules have been formulated by the editors of the Duden dictionary over the years (Heller, 1997: 9). The gist of the new proposals is to simplify those regulations, allowing more freedom for users. One of the main revisions is in the area of commas, which are no longer required before coordinating conjunctions such as *und/oder* (and/or) in order to separate two main clauses. (This is in accordance with error analyses which showed that in 70–80% of cases users were omitting such commas anyway – see Mentrup, 1998: 10). For example:

> *Der Schnee schmolz dahin(,) und bald ließen sich die ersten Blumen sehen(,) und die Vögel stimmten ihr Lied an.*

> (The snow was melting away and soon the first flowers could be seen and the birds began to sing.)

Widely criticised has been a further proposal that commas are no longer strictly required in some types of infinitive construction. This, it has been suggested, could lead to potential confusion in such phrases as *Ich rate ihm zu helfen* (I recommend that he helps/I recommend that he be helped). However, the guidelines clearly state that commas be used whenever the need arises to clarify such ambiguities (Heller, 1997: 9).

(6) Syllabification and word separation at the end of lines
(Worttrennung am Zeilenende)

Finally, a number of changes have been made to the way in which words can be separated at the ends of lines. Three traditional rules have been abandoned, namely that: (i) <st> should not be separated in words such as *We-ste* (waistcoat/vest); (ii) if <ck> were separated at the end of a line, then they should be converted to <kk>, as in *Zucker→Zuk-ker* (sugar); and (iii) it was incorrect to separate words resulting in a syllable of a single vowel as in *Ofen* (oven – inseparable). Thus, the following new forms are now possible: *Wes-te, Zuc-ker,* and *O-fen.*

Particularly problematic were discussions surrounding the hyphenation of foreign words, i.e. whether to prioritise etymology *(Heliko-pter)* or German users' own sense of syllable structure *(Helikop-ter)*. As with the spelling of foreign loans generally, no agreement could be reached and it was therefore decided to permit both variants.

(7) The extent of the reform

Described in the above detail, the proposed changes may easily give the impression of a significant intervention into the rules of German orthography. But just how much of the written language is actually implicated in the reform?

Quantifying the exact level of change has, of course, proved enormously problematic – does one count *types* (e.g. the hyphenation of all foreign loans as equivalent to one change in a given passage) or *tokens* (e.g. every single occurrence of a hyphenated loan in that passage)? And which bit of German does one consider anyway, given the impossibility of analysing the written language in its entirety?

Notwithstanding such methodological dilemmas, the most widely-quoted suggestion is that approximately 0.5% of the lexicon will be affected by the reform (excluding alterations to the <ß/ss> rule) (BVerfG, 14 July 1998b). In other words, the net effect of the reform is indisputably minimal. But as the press release by the *Kultusministerkonferenz* of 1 July 1996 clearly stated, the new regulations were never intended to constitute a comprehensive overhaul of German orthography, simply a harmonisation of the main inconsistencies which had not been clarified by the 1901/2 reform or had arisen as a result of language change occurring since that time.

The Constitutional Challenge

The previous section has demonstrated how certain interventions into German orthography were (and are) the source of ongoing debate. At least partly with this in mind, the Viennese Declaration of July 1996 recommended that the task of monitoring any unresolved issues, together with the future development of German orthography more generally, should fall to a newly-established 'Commission for German Spelling' (*Kommission für die deutsche Rechtschreibung*) based at the Institute for German Language (*Institut für deutsche Sprache* – IDS) in Mannheim. However, between 1996 and 1998, a level of opposition which by far exceeded that of isolated objections to specific structural aspects of the reform provoked a national dispute which, as indicated in the introduction, cast grave doubts over the feasibility of the reform *per se* (for documentation of press coverage during that time, see Zabel, 1996, 1997).

In late June 1996, Rolf Gröschner, professor of public law and legal philosophy at the University of Jena, took his protest against the reform to the Federal Constitutional Court (*Bundesverfassungsgericht*) in Karlsruhe (see BVerfG, 21 June 1996). Gröschner claimed that the new orthographic rules impinged upon his constitutional rights, as anchored in the German Basic Law (*Grundgesetz* – GG), in three main ways. First, since he would eventually be mocked for writing according to the old rules, Gröschner maintained that the reform was an affront to his personal dignity (Art. 1, §1 GG, *Menschenwürde*), his personal freedom (Art. 2, §1 GG – *Freiheit der Person*), and his freedom of action (Art. 2, §1 GG – *Handlungsfreiheit*). Second, he argued that children were traditionally taught the same orthography as their parents. However, given that his 15-year-old daughter would now be learning a different set of rules, the reform impinged upon his rights as a parent (*Elternrecht*) to educate his child as he thought fit (*Erziehungsrecht*), as enshrined in the section of the Basic Law dealing with marriage and family (Art. 6, §2 GG – *Ehe und Familie*). Finally, since he would not be permitted to mark the new spellings as incorrect in university examinations, Gröschner claimed that his freedom of opinion (*Meinungsfreiheit*) and freedom as a teacher (*Lehrfreiheit*) would also be curtailed (Art. 5, §3 GG).

Given that, in his opinion, basic constitutional rights were affected by the reform, Gröschner argued that a decree by the education ministers did not constitute an adequate legislative basis for its introduction. Instead, a parliamentary law was required, either via the *Bundestag* or the individual parliaments of the 16 *Länder* (for further details of this argument, see Gröschner, 1997; Gröschner & Kopke, 1997; Kopke, 1995, 1996, 1997). However, the Federal Constitutional Court did not agree. It rejected Gröschner's petition on all grounds, emphasising that such a contravention of constitutional rights could in any case only be substantiated retrospectively, i.e. some time after the reform had actually been introduced. Gröschner himself was undeterred. Whilst his 'top-down' approach had failed, he merely tackled the issue 'bottom-up', by offering legal support to many of the parents who went on to challenge the reform in a series of court cases at regional, i.e. *Länder,* level.

Between March 1997 and March 1998, 30 such regional cases were heard, the basis for which were broadly similar to Gröschner's original protest. The first to go against the reform was in Wiesbaden in July 1997, and this was followed by a further 11. Thus in a total of 12 out of 30 cases, judges agreed with plaintiffs that fundamental constitutional rights were indeed affected (see Mentrup, 1998: 2). At national level, however, prospects for the anti-reform campaign were less good: in December 1997, the Federal Constitutional Court ruled in accordance with its original rejection of Gröschner's petition in June 1996, maintaining once again that the reform was in fact within the legislative remit of the education ministers.

By the summer of 1998, the fate of the spelling reform hung in the balance, and would be decided in two ways: first, the ruling of the Federal Constitutional Court following a final hearing in May 1998; second, the outcome of a referendum to be held in September in Schleswig-Holstein, the most northerly Federal state. This was the result of a petition (*Volksbegehren*) which had gathered the requisite number of signatures stipulated by the regional constitution for a referendum to be held on this, or any other, issue (similar petitions in four other *Länder* failed to receive sufficient support).

In retrospect, it is probably no surprise that the Federal Constitutional Court stood by its initial rulings of June 1996 and December 1997, declaring once again that the reform did not impinge upon citizens' constitutional rights and was therefore within the remit of the education ministers (BVerfG, 14 July 1998a/b). As a result, the latter instructed schools across the country to go ahead with the reform as planned from 1 August 1998 (KMK, 31 July 1998). Interestingly, the Constitutional Court, anticipating the possibility of a 'no' vote in the Schleswig-Holstein referendum, also ruled that the agreement of all *Länder* was not in fact essential, and that the reform would still go ahead even if an individual *Land* chose to withdraw (see also KMK, 25 September 1998).

This was precisely what happened when, on 27 September 1998 (the same day as the Federal Elections), 56.4% of the population of Schleswig-Holstein voted against the introduction of the reform. The Social Democratic Minister for Education in Schleswig-Holstein, Gisela Böhrk, was then constitutionally obliged to repeal the introduction of the reform for all schools in that *Land*. Thus, from 1 November 1998, pupils who had been learning the new orthographic rules since 1996 would be required to learn (and, in some cases, re-learn) the old ones. Böhrk expressed her personal dismay at this decision, which, she believed, would merely confuse young people (Ewald, 1998). The referendum result also raised a number of other issues. For example, would schools in Schleswig-Holstein be required to provide separate textbooks exemplifying the old orthographic rules for their pupils, and could they afford to do so? What would be the impact of this 'no' vote regarding the general acceptance of the reform in all the other *Länder* and indeed German-speaking areas, where the reform is going ahead? And what would happen to pupils who moved between schools in Schleswig-Holstein and such areas?

Concluding Remarks

At the time of writing, it is too early to provide answers to questions such as those raised by the referendum in Schleswig-Holstein. It is nonetheless possible to reflect on the theoretical implications of the more general dispute over German orthographic reform from a sociolinguistic point of view.

In *Authority in Language,* James & Lesley Milroy (1999: 24–46) describe the so-called 'complaint tradition' surrounding English, which can be traced back to pronouncements by Swift on the alleged decline of the language in the early 18th century, and which continues up to the present day in the form of disputes over the teaching of standard English. According to the Milroys, such complaints by the public, the media, and sometimes even linguists themselves can be located within the broader framework of language standardisation. Thus, once a variety has undergone the preliminary stages of standardisation – characterised by selection, acceptance and diffusion of a standard norm – this needs to be followed by the *maintenance* of that norm via elaboration of function, the acquisition of prestige, codification, and prescription (ibid: 22–3). Complaints about various forms of perceived decline can therefore be seen as part of ongoing attempts to consolidate the prestige of a chosen standard in the face of language (and indeed social) change.

Although the Milroys discuss the complaint tradition primarily with reference to English, it need not surprise us that German – a language standardised to a similarly high degree, albeit only since the late 19th century – should also be subject to public altercations of the kind documented in this paper. Moreover, even though the processes of standardisation described by the Milroys relate primarily to *spoken* language, the role of *written* language cannot be underestimated, given that norms for standard spoken varieties are formulated largely on the basis of the written standard. When constituent elements of the written standard are then subjected to change, particularly via such *explicit* planning measures as the current reform of German orthography, it is hardly surprising that complainants are likely to feel that much more is at stake than merely the way in which a relatively small number of words are spelled. Indeed, it is the status and authority of the German standard in its entirety, which is thought to be in need of defence (for further discussion, see Johnson, in press). This goes some way towards explaining why so many Germans have been willing to take such extensive legal and political action over what might appear, to some, to be the rather trivial question of orthographic reform.

Where the German scenario described here offers an alternative perspective on the complaint tradition, and concomitant attempts to maintain the prestige of the standard, is in terms of the socio-cultural context in which it has occurred. Thus, the political configuration of the modern German state – not least its Federal structure and the pivotal role of the constitution in the lives of its citizens – render the German language subject to rather different types of complaint procedure than would be feasible in, for example, the UK. This, in turn, provides applied linguists not only with the opportunity to explore processes of standardisation and complaint within a different cultural context, but also means that an entirely different corpus of data becomes available as the basis for such work. It is to such data, particularly in the form of legal documentation, that I wish to turn my attention in the future.

References

*All documents and press releases where no publisher is listed are available on the web-site of the Institute for German Language in Mannheim (http://www. ids-mannheim.de/Rechtschreibreform).

Augst, G. and Schaeder, B. (1997) *Rechtschreibreform. Eine Antwort an die Kritiker.* Stuttgart: Klett.
Bundesverfassungsgericht (21 June 1996) *BVerfG, 1 BvR 1057/96 – Rechtschreibreform. Beschluß der 3. Kammer des Ersten Senats.*

Bundesverfassungsgericht (14 July 1998a) *BVerfG, 1 BvR 1640/97 – Rechtschreibreform. Urteil des Ersten Senats vom 14. Juli 1998.*

Bundesverfassungsgericht (14 July 1998b) Press release: *BVerfG: Erfolglose Verfassungsbeschwerde gegen 'Rechtschreibreform'.*

Denk, F. (1997) Eine der größten Desinformationskampagnen. In H.-W. Eroms and H. H. Munske (eds) *Die Rechtschreibreform: Pro und Kontra* (pp. 41–6). Berlin: Erich Schmidt Verlag.

Deutsche Rechtschreibung (1996) *Regeln und Wörterverzeichnis. Text der amtlichen Regelung.* Tübingen: Gunter Narr Verlag.

Eroms, H.-W. and Munske, H. H. (eds) (1997) *Die Rechtschreibreform: Pro und Kontra.* Berlin: Erich Schmidt Verlag.

Ewald, R. (28 September 1998) Sonderweg bei Schreibreform. In *Die Welt.*

Gröschner, R. (1997) Zur Verfassungswidrigkeit der Rechtschreibreform. In H.-W. Eroms and H. H. Munske (eds) *Die Rechtschreibreform: Pro und Kontra* (pp. 69–80). Berlin: Erich Schmidt Verlag.

Gröschner, R. and Kopke, W. (1997) Die 'Jensener Kritik' an der Rechtschreibreform. *Juristische Schulung* 4, 298–303.

Heller, K. (1997) Rechtschreibreform. In special extended January edition of *Sprachreport. Informationen und Meinungen zur deutschen Sprache.* Mannheim: Institut für deutsche Sprache.

Jansen-Tang, D. (1988) *Ziele und Möglichkeiten einer Reform der deutschen Orthographie seit 1901.* Frankfurt/Main: Lang.

Johnson, S. (in press) The Cultural Politics of the 1998 Reform of German Orthography. *German Life and Letters.*

Kopke, W. (1995) Rechtschreibreform auf dem Erlaßwege? *Juristenzeitung* 18, 874–80.

Kopke, W. (1996) *Rechtschreibreform und Verfassungsrecht.* Tübingen: Mohr.

Kopke, W. (1997) Ist die Rechtschreibreform noch zu stoppen? In H.-W. Eroms and H. H. Munske (eds) *Die Rechtschreibreform: Pro und Kontra* (pp. 111–6). Berlin: Erich Schmidt Verlag.

Kultusministerkonferenz (KMK) (30 November 1995) Press release: *Beschluß zur Neuregelung der deutschen Rechtschreibung.*

Kultusministerkonferenz (KMK) (1 July 1996) Press release: *Präsident der Kultusministerkonferenz unterzeichnet 'Gemeinsame Absichtserklärung' von Vertretern aus den deutschsprachigen Staaten und Gemeinschaften zur Neuregelung der deutschen Rechtschreibung.*

Kultusministerkonferenz (KMK) (31 July 1998) Press release: *Neuregelung der deutschen Rechtschreibung ab 1. August wirksam. Präsidentin der Kultusministerkonferenz zur Einführung der Rechtschreibreform.*

Kultusministerkonferenz (KMK) (25 September 1998) Press release: *Kein Stopp der neuen Rechtschreibung in den anderen Ländern.*

Küppers, H.-G. (1984) *Orthographiereform und Öffentlichkeit. Zur Entwicklung und Diskussion der Rechtschreibreformbemühungen zwischen 1876 und 1982.* Düsseldorf: Schwann.

Mentrup, W. (1998) *Neuregelung der Rechtschreibung. Zur Anhörung des Bundesverfassungsgerichtes (Karlsruhe 12. Mai 1998). Impressionen – Argumentationen.* Mannheim: Institut für deutsche Sprache.

Milroy, J. and Milroy, L. (1999) *Authority in Language.* London: Routledge. 3rd Edition.

Poschenrieder, T. (1997) S-Schreibung – Überlieferung oder Reform? In H.-W. Eroms and H. H. Munske (eds) *Die Rechtschreibreform: Pro und Kontra* (pp. 173–84). Berlin: Erich Schmidt Verlag.

Russ, C. V. J. (1994) *The German Language Today.* London: Routledge.
Sauer, W. W. and Glück, H. (1995) Norms and reforms: Fixing the form of the language. In P. Stevenson (ed.) *The German Language and the Real World* (pp. 69–93). Oxford: Clarendon Press.
Scheuringer, H. (1996) *Geschichte der deutschen Rechtschreibung. Ein Überlick.* Wien: Edition Praesens.
Wiener Absichtserklärung (1 July 1996) *Gemeinsame Absichtserklärung zur Neuregelung der deutschen Rechtschreibung.* (Reprinted in Heller, 1997: 11.)
Zabel, H. (1996) *Keine Wüteriche am Werk. Berichte und Dokumente zur Neuregelung der deutschen Rechtschreibung.* Hagen: Rainer Padligur Verlag.
Zabel, H. (1997) *Widerworte. 'Lieber Herr Grass, Ihre Aufregung ist unbegründet.' Antworten an Gegner und Kritiker der Rechtschreibreform.* Aachen: Shaker Verlag/AOL Verlag.

9 Women's Literacy in a Rural Pakistani Community

SHIRIN ZUBAIR
University of Cardiff

Abstract

This paper explores the uses and perceptions of literacy across genders and generations in a rural Pakistani community to demonstrate the way in which literacy relates to larger socio-cultural practices. The research reported here forms part of another study (in progress) which draws upon contemporary work by anthropologists and literacy researchers in different communities to show how identity impinges on literacy. The focus of this paper is women's literacy use. A brief discussion of the context of the research is followed by the presentation of data from focus groups. The data are used to suggest patterns of change across generations: the analysis is qualitative and interpretative. The emergent patterns and findings are discussed in the conclusion.

Introduction

My research draws upon Street's ideological model (1984) of literacy in which literacy is defined as shorthand for the social practices and conceptions of reading and writing. Within this framework, I analyse literacy practices as part of broader gender roles which relate to power in the family, home and community. Gender is not monolithic in any society: individuals of the same sex take on very different roles depending on class, education, occupation and situation (Heath, 1993). However, gender is an important component of an individual's identity. A cross-cultural approach to the study of gender is all the more interesting and illuminating because literacy is men's exclusive prerogative in some communities and women have limited access to certain types of literacy. In such communities, Besnier (1995) argues, the gendering of literacy is classically illustrated. Although Barton & Hamilton (1998) and Besnier (1995) take account of the gendered nature of literacy, research on literacy in women's everyday

114

lives in their communities is still very limited. Some research on women and literacy has been carried out in the United States and Canada by Rockhill (1993) and Horsman (1987) respectively. Rockhill, in her research on Hispanic immigrant women in America looked at literacy as a central issue in power dynamics between men and women. Literacy for these women carried with it the symbolic power of education, hence it posed a threat to power relations in the family. Horsman has looked at literacy-related issues in the lives of women from Nova Scotia. However, much remains to be explored and researched in this area with reference to third world countries like Pakistan, where women's literacy rate is often low (5–7% in rural communities).

In the present study, the focus is on gendered literacy practices, which are seen to be associated with the ideologies perpetuated by the dominant groups. I look at what women associate with various literacies by analysing group talk. In talking about their roles the women throw light on the significance and meanings of literacy in their day to day lives as well as the possible uses of various literacies. Before moving to these specifics, I want to make a few comments about the data which follow.

The research reported in this paper is part of a larger ethnographic study which looks at the distribution and uses of various literacies in the community, with special emphasis on women's literacy practices. The data consist of six focus group recordings, 45 interviews, fieldnotes, literacy documents and participant observation in literacy events, carried out in two adjoining villages in southern Punjab. The villages are situated at a distance of five miles from each other. The data collected have facilitated the creation of Table 1 (below) which illustrates the overall picture of various literacies in the community and of Table 2 which shows a more detailed picture of the distribution of the various literacies in women's lives.

Table 1 Literacies in two southern Punjab villages

Language	Domain	Uses
Arabic	Mosque	Religious
	Home	Religious
	Maktab	Religious
Urdu	Home	Entertainment
		Information
		Interactional
		Instrumental
		Confirmational

Table 1 *continued*

Language	Domain	Uses
	School	Medium/subject of instruction Official
	Workplace	Instrumental Official
	Street	Emblematic, i.e. billboards/graffiti/advertisements Propaganda, i.e. political/religious banners/posters
English	Home	Instrumental Entertainment Information
	School	Subject of study
	Workplace	Instrumental

Table 2 **Women's literacies**

Age	Language	Reading	Writing	Other
50–70	Arabic	Koran prayers		Teaching
	Urdu	newspapers tv calendars		Teaching
30–49	Arabic	Koran prayers		Teaching
	Urdu	newspapers magazines calendars cards/letters tv	letters diaries record-keeping signing legal documents	
15–29	Arabic	Koran prayers		Teaching

Table 2 *continued*

Age	Language	Reading	Writing	Other
	Urdu and English	newspapers magazines novels medicine labels cards/letters calendars	letters diaries record-keeping messages notes exam papers signing legal papers/cheques poetry short stories	Teaching Studying

Women: Lives and literacies

The most prominent use of literacy in women's lives in the community is that of the oral recitation of the Koran, which increases during the month of *Ramadan*. Most people in the village read the Koran either daily or occasionally. Most women, particularly from the old and middle groups, daily read the Koran in the early hours of dawn after the *fajjar* prayers (see Appendix for glossary). The purpose of recitation of the Koran is not to understand the meanings, but to perform a pious religious ritual. The ritual prayers are also offered in Arabic five times a day. Men go to the village mosque five times a day to offer ritual prayers called *namaz*, and women offer these prayers at home. Although much of what they read in the Koran and *namaz* is not understood by the people, the ritualistic readings have a strong symbolic significance and meaning for them. The act of reading is symbolic of the assertion and confirmation of their religious identity and beliefs.

Women also read other religious material, for example booklets in Urdu, to gain guidance and information about the code and performance of various rituals like *namaz, roza, zakat* and *haj*, which form the basics of Islamic faith. Traditionally, women's access to literacy acquisition was limited to Arabic literacy. Therefore, a vast majority of the older women can either only read the Koran, or read Arabic and some Urdu, e.g. newspaper headlines, names on cards, television announcements etc. However, the middle and younger group of women who can read and write Urdu and Urdu and English respectively, engage themselves in a wide variety of literacy practices ranging from reading bills and medicine labels to the reading of fiction and creative writing. The gendering of literacy practices manifests itself in women typically reading the electricity bills and writing records of household accounts, whereas the payment of bills and shopping for the house is done by the men in the family.

In the remainder of the paper, using extracts from two focus group inter- actions, I illustrate the perceptions of the community with reference to literacy acquisition and use, across genders and generations. The participants in the group are from the landowning class. There are six women and one man (who dropped in by chance during the recording). Following Gee (1990) and Horsman (1987), the paper focuses on the way that language frames reality and shapes how we see ourselves in the world. Horsman (1987) and Barton & Hamilton (1998) have analysed excerpts, phrases and words from interview data to show how people talk about literacy and illiteracy in their lives. My analysis follows this approach. In the examples below the people are symbolised as follows:

S, R & O = Older women   A = Woman in her 30s

Z & N = Younger women   M = Moderator is myself

F = Male participant in early 40s

The transcription conventions used will be found in the Appendix. The aim in analysing the content and form of these extracts, is to explore and illustrate: (a) what literacy means to users of various generations and genders (b) how the gender role ideologies restrict women's access to certain literacies (c) how identity and power are negotiated through talk.

Example 1

038. **R:** [yes absolutely there was *izzat*–if someone came outside we

039. **O:** [very respectable people

040. **R:** couldn't tell whether it was a human being or an animal we

041. **R:** remained indoors like silent birds–<u>now</u> there's freedom children

042. **R:** are also being educated and we also have some awareness but

043. **R:** for us those times were okay=

044. **O:** =it was good=

045. **R:** =it was absolutely fine

046. **O:** (unclear)

047. **R:** those times were absolutely fine those elders did right now

048. **R:** there's freedom–children have an easy life now even for us its

049. **R:** easier

050. **M:** umm would you tell me something about it? (signalling towards
      younger participants)

051. **A:** what do we know? [what shall we (unclear)

052. **Z:**   [I think that there shouldn't be so many=

053. **A:** =restrictions=

054. **Z:** =restrictions should not be there because__(starts speaking Urdu)

055. **Z:** one can't sit at home (**M:** umm) that's our view because the new

056. **Z:** generation (laughs) would say that one can't sit at home there

057. **Z:** should be some freedom–at least to move about to meet friends

058. **Z:** to go out with friends to parks to see movies–there should be a

059. **Z:** little bit of freedom- too much of it (restrictions) is not good

060. **Z:** (**M:** umm) I think if there is too much pressure on a girl she

061. **Z:** won't be able to do what's right for her (**M:** umm) that's all

062. **Z:** (laughs)

Example 2

164. **M:** why didn't you?

165. **F:** it's okay if women are literate they become very free Islam is

166. **F:** about strictly observing *purdah purdah* is obligatory a woman

167. **F:** must cover herself if she goes out head must be covered it is

168. **F:** Islamic [Islam

169. **S:**   [(laughs) see

170. **F:** these are the Islamic rules=

171. **S:** =(jokingly) he is our Islamic=

172. **F:** =Islam says teach up to this learn to read that you are familiar

173. **F:** with the religion but people forget religion and pay attention to

174. **F:** worldly education more they have [no respect for elders

175. **N:**   [yeah this is also this is

176. **N:** written meaning that our prophet said that even if you have to

177. **N:** go to China to get educated you should go this means some

178. **N:** freedom was given=

179. **F:** =China that

180. **N:** this is all made up by them to suppress to kill that 'you aren't

181. **N:** going out you aren't learning literacy' when Islam allows one

182. **N:** to go out to become literate then these these restrictions are

183. **N:** imposed by man

Language Analysis

Lexis and metaphor

Analysis of the lexis and figures of speech in these samples reveals antithetical juxtapositions of concepts and attitudes; for example antonyms like *restrictions/ pressure/suppress* versus *freedom, old* versus *new, then* versus *now.* These collocations are emblematic of the various strands of thought exemplified by different generational and gender groups in the talk. If we accept a Bakhtinian perspective, where language is seen as a site of contest for power struggles between different groups in the community (Dentith, 1995), the use of these antonyms seems to reflect conflicting ideologies. They show the participants' preoccupation with these concepts and emphasise the fact that the people in the community are caught between opposing ideologies, and the notion of women's literacy is inextricably intertwined with these sharp contrasts.

As an example of the use of figurative language, I will discuss the metaphors *silent birds* (by R in line 41) and *caged birds* (elsewhere in the data). These words are said in a rather non-emotive, neutral and dispassionate tone; in fact, the women are partly praising the traditions of their parents and elders, thus reiterating and subconsciously reinforcing the dominant ideologies of the community. One could argue, however, that the fact that they use such strong and powerful images to describe their peculiar predicament and their literacy histories reflects some kind of underlying complaint. These women who see themselves and their peers as *caged* and *silent birds* have used a very telling image for domesticated women who are deprived of their basic rights. Their voices were silenced: an apt image for their lifelong silence. Although not apparent here, there is a consistent use of the passive voice in expressing themselves and narrating their literacy histories which strengthens the point that these women were not active agents in decision-making about their own lives but rather passive recipients of other's decisions. The use of the metaphors *silent birds* and *caged bird* reflects an enforced silence. In a wider context Kaplan (1990: 312) observes:

A very high proportion of women's poems are about the right to speak and write ... that larger subject, the exploration and definition of gender difference in culture, it becomes a distinct issue when women speak or write, and men protest, not only or primarily at what they say, but at the act itself.

Thus the metaphors *caged birds* and *silent birds* epitomise the older women's peculiar predicament in that they had absolutely no contact with the outside world. Although a *caged bird* is restricted in its movement it can still sing and its voice can reach out to ears outside its confines, whereas these women are *silent* as well as *caged birds* as they are not even heard: their voices are muffled and choked within the confines of their homes. Hence it is a social silence they are complaining about here.

Pronouns

I would like to argue that the 'collective literacy voice' of the older women's generation serves as a contrast to the younger women's individualism. Their use of the pronouns *we* and *I* respectively, serve as indicators of the change in their perceptions of their own roles and identities. The younger women's use of *I* and awareness of their rights in terms of their access to Urdu and English literacies is a reflection of their changing roles. The middle group woman, A, also uses the plural pronoun *we* thus speaking for the entire group, but when Z speaks, she uses the pronoun *I*: this gives her a definite voice of her own, a definite personal identity, an individuality as opposed to the collective voice of the older women. In lines 54–56, however, she uses a plural pronoun which makes it clear that she sees herself as a representative of the younger generation as opposed to the older women. Similarly, in other parts of the transcript, N also uses *I* instead of *we*. Her views on literacies are clearly very modern. However, she also uses the plural pronoun *our* when she refers to the entire community, as in *our prophet* (line 176), because she is referring to their collective identity as Muslims.

In the second sample, when questioned about not sending his daughter to school, F's response is spontaneous: *if women are literate they become very free. They* here refers to the women, the other group as opposed to the self. Seeing women as *they* has implications: he regards them as the other group struggling for power and dominance through literacy. *We* and *they* are then two polarities, two groups in competition, and the *we* group is more powerful than *they* and whether knowingly or unknowingly, does not want to give up its control and power over the other group. Wales (1996) observes that in semiotic and semantic terms, generalised *we* and *they* are in binary opposition to each other, i.e. positive v. negative, functioning as value-laden antonyms. In a social and ideological rather than literal sense, *we* can mean a collective identity like a Greek chorus, which is what, I would argue, it means here, irrespective of the individualism of some participants.

Content Analysis

A close reading of the two samples suggests that the gender roles in the community are undergoing a process of redefinition and renegotiation. The change, however, is unobtrusive and gradual. This is demonstrated by almost all the participants, including the man, by showing an ambivalence at times when talking about women's literacy and the change it brings or might bring. Secondly, having internalised the traditional ideologies and expectations in terms of the gender roles, the participants do not know how to replace these by alternative ideologies, hence the ambivalence and uncertainty in their answers.

It is clear from other parts of the discussions that the older women view literacy acquisition in relation to better marriage prospects, the men view it as only peripheral in a woman's life, the younger women are the only group in the community who are in a process of challenging and questioning the dominant ideologies regarding sex roles. However, most of them also still feel obliged to fulfil the expected roles rather than go for self-realisation. This is partly due to their socialisation into and internalisation of these roles from very early on in their lives and partly due to the absence of an alternative goal and role.

The younger women express their own views about the value of literacy by emphasising the fact that literacy can offer independence, higher education, equal rights and job opportunities for women. For example in another part of the transcript, N expresses her opinions about languages and language learning. She thinks that all languages are worth learning and it is worthwhile to learn literacy in different languages of the world rather than confine literacy only to Arabic. She holds strong views about female education and literacy and exhibits a sharp 'critical literacy awareness' (Wallace's term, 1989). Z Shares N's stance that there are no restrictions on female literacy or education in Islam. Like N, she categorically denies what F has to say. Thus 'critical literacy awareness' is quite evident among the younger participants along with a sense of individualism and awareness of their rights. Both Z and N (lines 52–62, 175–83) question and challenge the dominant male values of the entire community by challenging and arguing with F who assumes the role of a representative of the male members of the community. They want equal opportunities of education, equal rights and equal status with the men in the community. Elsewhere, when asked by the Moderator whether she would like to study more, Z gave a very interesting answer. On the one hand she said she was keen on education, and on the other was playing the role of an obedient daughter in her family: a daughter who gave up her studies to look after her mother and who happily accepted the family's decision regarding her marriage.

Conclusion

The data under discussion are suggestive of the juxtaposition of threatening and non-threatening, powerful and powerless forms of literacy. The metaphors *caged* and *silent birds* refer not only to women's peculiar predicament regarding their lives and literacies, they actually refer to the act of speech. There is the ideology of the threat that literacy may pose in the present discussion: the male participant caught unawares, time and again uses the pronouns *we* and *they/them*, as in, *if we educate women, they become free.*

The tension between the unequal and arbitrary use of power and the threat of certain types of literacy underlie the discourse. As no threat is inherent in Koranic literacy, the women are allowed access to it. It is a non-threatening form of literacy therefore acceptable to the dominant segments of the community. The threatening forms of literacy are not acceptable to the dominant group in the community, hence the gatekeeping around Urdu and English literacies.

The debate between F and N about women's literacy in Islam makes it clear that the acquisition or non-acquisition of literacy is tied to the tradition of *purdah* and to the community's interpretations of the sex roles in Islam. The concept of secular literacy is constructed in the discourse as an empowering phenomenon. Literacy carries with it a promise but also fear and threat. It holds the promise of economic and financial gains as well as independence, hence it is desirable. It is a threat because it empowers the individual, hence the control over women's access to it. It is to be feared because it implies change in the old system and adaptation to new identities and roles. Gal (1998) in her research on sex roles and language change in a bilingual community in Austria, found that the young women are more willing to participate in social change and in the linguistic change which symbolises it. A similar finding emerges from my data analysis: the younger women are no longer re-enacting the roles of the *silent* and *caged birds*. They do raise their individual voices to be heard. They are in the process of redefining and renegotiating these roles but simultaneously trying not to break away from the community by being willing to accept some of the traditional behaviour patterns and decisions.

Through my analysis, I hope to have shown that the value and promise of literacy is not understood uniformly by the participants but varies among different age groups and individuals. The difference between women's and men's perceptions of literacies is at the heart of the matter. The practices and uses of literacy in an individual's life, depend on their socialisation into the institutions and values of their community which might include constraints and responsibilities association with gender, age, social and family roles.

Appendix

Transcription conventions: Key to symbols used

[simultaneous or overlapping utterance

=   contiguous utterances

( )   1. unclear utterances

        2. description of non-verbal activity e.g laughs

–   short pause

__   long pause

?   functional question

' '   in narrative passages involving reported speech inverted commas are used
        to establish the provenance of an utterance

<u>line</u>   emphasis

Glossary

namaz   = ritual prayers offered five times daily

fajjar   = pre-dawn prayers

roza   = fast

zakat   = alms

haj   = pilgrimage to Mecca

purdah   = screen; segregation of sexes

izzat   = honour

ramadan = Muslims' holy month of fasting

maktab   = a mosque-school for boys

References

Barton, D. and Hamilton, M. (1998) *Local Literacies: Reading and writing in one community.* London: Routledge.
Besnier, N. (1995) *Literacy, Emotion and Authority.* Cambridge: Cambridge University Press.
Dentith, S. (1995) *Bakhtinian Thought: An introductory reader.* London, New York: Routledge.
Gal, S. (1998) Peasant men can't get wives: Language change and sex roles in a bilingual community. In J. Coates (ed.) *Language and Gender: A reader.* Oxford: Blackwell.

Gee, J. (1990) *Social Linguistics and Literacies: Ideologies in discourses.* London, New York and Philadelphia: Falmer.

Heath, S. B. and Mclaughlin, M. W. (eds) (1993) *Identity and Inner-city Youth: Beyond ethnicity and gender.* New York: Teachers College Press.

Horsman, J. (1987) *Something in My Mind Besides the Everyday: Women and literacy.* Toronto: Women's Press.

Kaplan, C. (1990) Language and gender. In D. Walder (ed.) *Literature in the Modern World: Critical essays and documents.* New York and Oxford: Open University Press.

Rockhill, K. (1993) Gender language and the politics of literacy. In B. V. Street (ed.) *Cross-cultural Approaches to Literacy.* Cambridge: Cambridge University Press.

Street, B. V. (1984) *Literacy in Theory and Practice.* Cambridge: Cambridge University Press.

Wales, K. (1996) *Personal Pronouns in Present-day English.* Cambridge, New York and Australia: Cambridge University Press.

Wallace, C. (1992) Critical literacy awareness. In N. Fairclough (ed.) *Critical Language Awareness.* London: Longman.

10 Issues for a Working Agenda in Literacy

GUNTHER KRESS
Institute of Education, University of London

Abstract

Everyone knows about the challenges facing all of us who have an interest in literacy, wherever our main focus of attention happens to be: social, technological, cultural, economic, representational, theoretical. All of us are dealing with many or some of these issues in the course of our work. Academic life being what it is, we are left to deal with them in often fragmentary ways, which obscure connections, gaps, or the need for reformulation. In this talk I wish to address some of these issues in an attempt to work away from fragmentation, and towards the possibility of integration. Two issues I want to deal with specifically are those of theoretical divergences and the ensuing problems; and the changing 'real world' of representation and the consequences for thinking about communication. In relation to the first I want to ask about the scope of theories, and where their strengths and their limits might lie; in relation to the second I want to suggest that we need to move away from reliance on the notion of literacy (or even the plural literacies) alone and begin to investigate what I shall call 'communicational webs', their characteristics and their social (and other) dimensions and environments.

Domains of Work: What do we need to do the job?

I have this small text/object here, a small card with printed language on it, and I want to know what I need to be able to say about it in order to give a reasonably comprehensive account of its meaning, and how that meaning is produced.

ITALIAN LEATHER

ANNAPELLE

Annapelle is a 100% Australian owned company specialising in the manufacture and importing of quality handcrafted Leather handbags and accessories.

This fine produce which is made in Italian Leather was manufactured in the Peoples Republic of China under strict supervision, and the packaging and quality inspection was carried out in Melbourne, Australia.

MADE IN CHINA

Figure 1

My interest might be oriented in an analytic, descriptive interpretative direction; or it might be oriented more in the direction of questions such as: what resources of representation, in what organisation, make this text what it is?

The provenance of this text is Australian, circa 1996; it came as one of three cards (the size of a business card or a credit card, roughly) inserted in a small leather purse, sent from Australia as a present; no doubt as a small memento from 'home'.

That is one way of talking about this textual object. I now want to look at it from a number of different perspectives. I am of course focused on the issue of 'literacy' first and foremost: the theme of the conference at which I am giving this talk; and equally I am aware of the larger context which is the frame for this conference, that of Applied Linguistics. So from this perspective let me look at linguistic features: those around discursive organisation; those around grammar/ syntax; punctuation; and aesthetic aspects of linguistic text – stylistic/poetic features.

This is not the place for a detailed analysis (I simply want to indicate what kinds of things our account will need to include), but even a superficial reading indicates that the discourses which seem at work here are those around *national-ism* (the emphasis on Australianness; on Australian ownership; on the incorpora-tion of Australian values and practices); *racism* perhaps, and certainly ethnic difference (the nervousness about standards of manufacture in China; and by contrast the positive evaluation of European manufacture and Australian quality assurance); *aesthetics/taste* (the evaluative adjective *fine*; the valuation given to mode of production: *handcrafted*); *economics and business* (the 'jargon' of contemporary practice: *quality inspection* etc.); and *heritage* (the invocation of Europe as Italianness; etc). This rests on more than the mere mention of topics, but rests on the manner of the respective evaluation of these factors in hierarchies or webs of value.

As I will indicate these discourses are realised in a number of linguistic features, and in other representational modes. As two instances take on the one hand the relative clause 'which is made in Italian leather', and within that, on the other hand, the preposition *in* ('in Italian leather'). This relative clause 'should be' a non-restrictive relative clause, but is here treated as a restrictive relative clause (the contrast between 'a star, which, like most of the others, isn't visible until it is quite dark' and 'the star which outshines every other in the early evening sky'). The latter makes the object named by the headnoun unique; the former doesn't. Now we can assume that the usage here is 'ungrammatical'; but I want to suggest that it is part of a whole ensemble of features working in one overall ideological direction, of which 'uniqueness of the product' in this specific respect, is an essential component. The preposition 'in' of 'made in Italian leather' similarly strikes me – or struck me at first reading – as odd. My feeling was, as that of others on whom I have tried this, that the 'normal' preposition would or should have been *of* or *from*: made 'of' from Italian Leather'. But in gives this clause a very specific 'feel' – derived from its qualities as 'container' metaphor, to use the Lakoff/Johnson parlance (Lakoff & Johnson, 1980). We are precisely, metaphorically 'in' a world of craft, of quality, of tradition, of leather. The prepositional usage, as much as that of the relative clause, is part of the realisational apparatus for the discursive/ideological effects aimed for here. Discourse reaches into, draws on, organises all features of language – or better, speakers and writers do, in this aim of achieving discursive/ideological effects (see Hodge & Kress, 1979/1992; Kress, 1984/89; Fairclough, 1989, 1992).

Punctuation is, similarly, drawn into the service of discursive realisation (as well as into the aesthetic, which itself, is of course, not 'outside' the ideological/discursive domain). My linguistic pedant's punctuation would be, roughly this.

Annapelle is a 100% Australian owned company, specialising in the manufacture and importing of quality handcrafted Leather handbags and accessories. This fine product, which is made in Italian Leather, was manufactured in the Peoples' Republic of China, under strict supervision, and the packaging and quality inspection was carried out in Melbourne, Australia.

In the original, which is, in my view, severely underpunctuated, there are just two commas: and each serves, I feel certain, specific discursive purposes. The first comma separates 'production in China' from 'quality inspection and packaging in Australia'; that is, it marks precisely the split between 'us' and 'them', the 'safe' and the 'doubtful', the ethnically secure from the ethnically problematic. The second comma separates the names of two geographical locations, and by doing this gives us 'Australianness' twice – compared with the single, semantically 'fused' 'Melbourne Australia', without a comma. My reason for feeling quite secure about this reading of punctuation is the sparseness of the original, which foregrounds punctuation where it is used. In my view the sparseness is aimed at achieving an aesthetic effect – the *look* of a clear, uncluttered, unfussy text. The text as punctuated by me might satisfy a pedant's heart; it does nothing to enhance the look of the text.

As I mentioned, the aesthetic is of course entirely within the discursive/ideological: producing a 'beautiful' textual object is precisely to make the discourse of the aesthetic into a foregrounded one – with all its attendant meanings of 'care for the beautiful', in its manifold ramifications for the commodity and for the producer of both commodity and textual object. This is particularly essential when the distinctive economic contribution of the Australian company lies in the area of semiotic 'services' – packaging being one of the two. The layout of the original text is in accord with and realises the demands of this discourse: the text is sculpted to produce a pleasing shape. It is, for me, reminiscent of 17th century poets such as Herbert and their use of layout to achieve specific aesthetic sculptured effects. These aesthetic features are of course of one piece with the evocation of certain tastes by 'Italian Leather' and its association of European culture, (Renaissance) Florence, etc.

'Taste' and the manufacture, here, of 'taste' is a linguistic/semiotic task: it produces, from a linguistic/textual perspective, a certain kind of reader, and a certain kind of audience. From the perspective of commodity production, advertising, marketing, it produces a certain consumer, and a certain kind of market. The semiotic/linguistic/textual/ideological accomplishment here lies in the seamless bringing together of these diverse discourses through their multiple realisation, into a plausible semiotic/ideological whole which can serve to produce readers/consumers who see themselves as social and cultural subjects appropriately addressed by this configuration.

Perhaps I should ask the question at this point: am I 'doing' Applied Linguistics in this, am I safely within its ambit, and within that of literacy? My own answer would be yes, certainly. These are linguistic resources, (even 'layout' is) and I am discussing their use and deployment in relation to the interests of the maker of the text.

I said that language was not the only semiotic mode involved. The card as material object is semiotically significant, perhaps as significant as the linguistic. But if it might be objected that considerations of layout are stretching the boundaries of Applied Linguistics, then a concern with typeface, logo, colour, type of paper used in the card, etc. might seem to move us out of the domain of Applied Linguistics, into the domain of some other discipline's concern – 'communication' perhaps, or semiotics. Of course the question is, are we still 'in' literacy. My own view is that with the shift in focus to the *materiality of the representational means* we remain in the vicinity, at least, of literacy. As far as Applied Linguistics is concerned any answer at this point would be: we have left concern with and focus on the semiotic mode of language, hence we are 'out' of Applied Linguistics in that respect. As I will say in a moment, however, we have not left concern with language in the sense that the use of other semiotic modes in communication has direct and specific effects on the use – and on the characteristics of language.

This is a difficult and important debate about disciplinary boundaries, theories, their extent and usefulness, and 'pay-offs' in application. I won't say much about this except to attempt a broad distinction which may prove useful in my further discussion, and perhaps in further work and thinking generally.

The distinction I want to make is between the focus on the materiality of semiotic modes, and their historically developed cultural shape as representational resources, and the work, the action, the practices with and around these resources, in which these resources are constantly, incessantly remade. The first of these, the materiality, I shall talk about as a concern with 'the stuff' of literacy; the second is already spoken of as concern with 'events', 'practices'. In the discussion of the Annapelle example it is impossible not to focus on the materiality in several different ways; it is equally impossible not to focus on the 'events', 'the practices' which have given rise to the use of the resources in this particular way, and which lead to their constant reshaping.

Of course, by 'stuff' I mean the material both in its physical sense – speech as sound, for instance, or writing as visual – as well as material in a more abstract sense, so that I will speak of the stuff of 'lexis' without (necessarily) thinking of the sound-shape of a word, or the stuff of syntax, without (necessarily) thinking of the possible visual or graphic display of the element of syntax. But both kinds of materiality are there in this notion of stuff. It is my name for everything which is available as material for human (and therefore) social semiosis. Materiality brings us directly to 'body', and insists that we can never treat representational resources as merely abstract: language-as-speech has regularity, order, structure, which can be thought about and represented abstractly; it is also entirely bodily, as sound, even though sound in that physical materiality, in the production or reception of sound in/by the body it is entirely semioticised.

This is not therefore a reinvention of the old form – content distinction; on the contrary it is an attempt to overcome it. It is a distinction of the *materiality of resources* (always meaningful) and of the *work performed* with, the *action performed* with these materials.

Let me give two instances of this idea of 'stuff' and of the work performed on it. One concerns the move by two three-year olds into the writing systems of their cultures; the other concerns the use of colour as a semiotic mode.

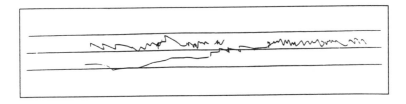

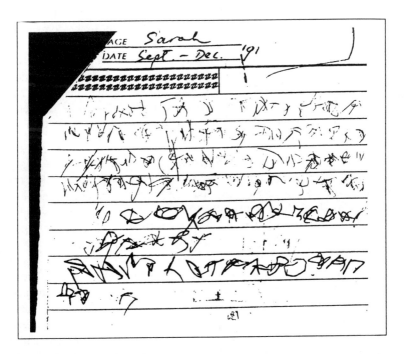

Figure 2 Alphabetic script (top) / logographic script (bottom)

The two girls, one from an 'alphabetic' culture, and one from a 'logographic/ ideographic' one, are both dealing with 'stuff' in both senses. Seen abstractly, they are figuring out the 'logic' of the writing system of their cultures, and producing their sense of the logic of the organisation of the 'stuff', a sense of what the meaning of each of the two scriptorial systems is. Seen from the bodily and the physical, they enact the logic which they have deduced materially, physically, bodily, as real actions on a real material surface. In this process neuromuscular pathways are established, the tactility of writing is experienced, and each system in its physical materiality and in its more abstract materiality is *embodied*, literally, in neuro-muscular action. (I have discussed these examples more fully, for instance in Kress 1997).

Let me turn to the example of colour. The examples I have in mind come from two 'Home Magazines' – one *Maison Française* (Numéro Été, 1996) and one *Home Flair* (November 1997). Both make colour-as-semiotic mode a feature on their front pages. The theme of *Maison Française* (as announced on its front page) is Rêve d'été, and it is about 'choosing well': Bien choisir: des meubles mobiles, des tapis végétaux, des rotins malins, des tables de jardin; and 'living well': Bien vivre: Les plaisirs de la douche, le charme des vérandas, les nouvelles maisons en bois. It is about Du soleil, de l'ombre, de l'eau, de l'aire, du bleu, du blanc. *Home Flair* has as its theme (its 'cover look') 'dreaming in colour, a country kitchen with a modern taste'. It is the focus on *bleu* and *blanc* (in the context of the other features) in the French magazine which attracted my attention initially. (In the case of *Home Flair* the colours are distinctly different – browns, yellows, oranges, blue, some green.) In one feature in *Maison Française* 'Le Bleu du Ciel', blue is the dominant colour: 'Entre ciel et mer une couleur s'impose tout naturellement: le bleu. Serein mais dynamique, il encadre, relie, souligne l'architecture pure et dure de cette maison ...' (p. 131).

Now this too is representational materiality: the questions are: 'Is this semiotically organised?' (that is, has it a cultural history which has made it into a representational resource; and 'How does this work?' Using the categories put forward by Michael Hoey in his talk at this conference we can ask: 'is there cohesion?'; 'is there collocation?' 'is there colligation?', and ask too his quoted question of John Sinclair's: 'does it have rules that could be broken?'; 'could you have ill-formed structures?' The answer is 'yes, absolutely!' Both in the French and in the English magazine there is cohesion: colours, whether the bleu or the blanc, occur across the space of a page, a double-page spread, and across the eight pages of the feature as a cohesive link; and they spill over into a linked feature 'L'été. En toute simplicité', where it is bleu and blanc as semiotic feature which provide the major cohesive device both within this feature and with the preceding one. Is there collocation: 'yes', equally clearly. The colour-scheme of both features (though each is differently selective) provides a collocational set, as clearly as that of any text, or of any text in a specific register. Is there colligation, that is, are there clearly active links over greater spans? Again, clearly 'yes'. And are there rules that could be broken?: 'Yes, absolutely'. All one needs to do is to interleaf a page from the French with the English magazine, or vice-versa, and the breaking of the rules (and therefore the clarity of the rule system) is absolutely apparent. Certain colours 'go with' the bleu and the blanc (and the browns and oranges of *Home Flair*), and some absolutely don't.

There is also cohesion across modes: I won't focus on this here, (both magazines do), but it is clear that the semiotic mode of *colour* coheres with *texture* as semiotic mode in specific ways, and collocates with *shape* as semiotic mode, with *pattern,* with materials such as rock, wood, earthenware, etc. In the English magazine the checks of the cloth of the curtain and tablecloth 'go with' the turned legs of chair and table, etc. etc.

My point in having the short quotation from *Maison Française* is to make the point (not to develop it here) that these semiotic modes 'go with' language: there is coherence across modes as much as within; and the discursive organisation expressed in language is also expressed in colour, texture, shape. le bleu 'serein mais dynamique, il encadre, relie, souligne l'architecture pure et dure ...' In fact, in the way it is expressed here, the mode of colour is the foregrounded semiotic means for the realisation of the discourses around 'living', 'life-style' which are at work here. Language here has a backgrounded role: it comments on, it frames, it underlines; it is not in the centre.

This is my point in saying that in moving to the consideration of other semiotic modes our focus has moved from language, and maybe, therefore, we are 'out' of Applied Linguistics. We are, however, absolutely involved in considerations around the communicational and representational functions of language; and of their effects on how language as semiotic mode is changed.

To return to my first example briefly: I can now ask about the significance of the colour of the Annapelle card, which is a kind of olivey/eucalyptus green. Is it significant? does it cohere with and realise the discourses?, and does it work with the overall ideological effect produced by their conjunction in this particular ensemble? 'Yes, of course'. This green is able to collocate with Italian-ness and with Australian-ness; it 'goes with' the brown of Italian leather, and with the specific taste realised in that. Of course, there is an alternative to realising Australian-ness in colour: not the eucalypt-green of this card ('the colour of the Australian bush'), but the red-gold-black of the Australian (Aboriginal) flag. But the discourses invoked by and realised by that colour combination would not be coherent with the discourses invoked by the language: it would be breaking the semiotic/cultural rules, it would produce an 'ungrammatical' textual entity. Or at least it would do so here: it could of course be used precisely to unsettle the linguistically realised discourses; and to evoke the possibility of others. In the context of the need to produce a market for a commodity, this would not seem a sensible procedure.

This is what I mean by a focus on 'stuff'. It enables me to think usefully about what it is that I do and that others do. I think I work more on the 'stuff' side, with a keen eye on practices. Others work right in the middle; yet others work on the 'practices' side, with an eye on the 'stuff'. For me it is essential to think about practices, because work produces change – whether physical work on physical materiality, or 'mental' work on abstract materiality; it is work on and with stuff which produces changes in the shape of the stuff. The constantly transformative, agentive work of humans – shaped by their interest and expressive of their interest – produces what we recognise as the regularities, and what we call the systems of grammar, of phonology, and as I would wish to insist, of all semiotic modes.

The Social and the Political Environment of Work in Literacy

The third topic in this paper poses the question *'literacy' and/or 'communication'*. Before I move to that, I wish to ask some questions about the wider social, economic, cultural environment in which 'literacy practices' take place. This is essential for us to understand the extent to which our work, our theorising, is shaped by forces active on us, in our environment; and it is essential if we wish to take an active role in the shaping of that environment.

If we need to set our frame of thinking and of working more widely than we have done hitherto, is that because of a misrecognition so far of the essential scope, or is it because the world around us is changing the environment of representation and communication, forcing us into rethinking, theorising newly. In my view it is largely the latter, though it is of course possible then to look back at present and past understandings and work, and see that newly also.

The representational world of the 1990s is different to that of the 1960s. If one compares a newspaper from 1996 with its version in 1966 the difference will be starkly apparent: the latter is (still) truly one of the print-media: printed language covers the front-page. In 1996 the 'same' newspaper will be covered in images, print will be mainly large screamer headlines, and printed language will make up a very small proportion of the page. In 1966 the television news consisted largely of an image of a 'newsreader' reading written scripts of the news. In the 1996 TV there are not newsreaders, but newspresenters; the TV news is largely visual with spoken language as a commentary and framing rather than as the central communicational means.

My example of two school text-books makes this point. The time-space between them is 50 years, but the point remains.

76   MAGNETISM AND ELECTRICITY

the magnetic poles. Fig. 62(c) shows the combined field of (a) and (b) when the wire is placed between the poles.

Note that, in Fig. 62(a) and (b), the lines of force on the left of the wire are in the same direction as those of the external field, while those on the right of the wire are in the opposite direction. Consequently in the combined field of Fig. 62(c) the field to the left of the wire is strong—there are a large number of lines, while the field to the right is weak.

If we assume, with Faraday, that the lines of force are in tension and trying to shorten (see p. 18), we should expect the wire to be urged to the right. This is precisely what we find by experiment.

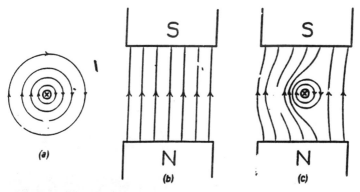

Fig. 62. (a) Magnetic field due to current in straight wire. (b) Field due to magnetic poles. (c) Combined field of (a) and (b).

The principle of the electric motor.

The simple electric motor consists of a coil pivoted between the poles of a permanent magnet (see Fig. 63). When a current is passed through the coil in the direction indicated in the figure we can show, by applying Fleming's left-hand rule, that the left-hand side of the coil will tend to move down and the right-hand side to move up. (Remember that the direction of the field due to the permanent magnet is from the N. to the S. pole.) Thus the coil will rotate in a counter-clockwise direction to a vertical

Figure 3 1938 Science text (McKenzie)

12·9 *Electronics*

Circuits

In your first circuits you used torch bulbs joined with wires. Modern electrical equipment uses the same basic ideas. But if you look inside a computer there are not many wires or torch bulbs. The wires and bulbs have been replaced by electronic devices like transistors, chips and light-emitting diodes.

Transistors and chips are examples of *semi-conductors*. They are made from special crystals like silicon. Transistors work because they only conduct electricity in the right conditions. They are useful because they can turn on and off very fast, and they need very little electricity.

An electronic light

● You can make electronic circuits with wires like the circuits you made before. The difficulty is that the contacts are poor, and sometimes things do not work. It is far better to *solder* the components.

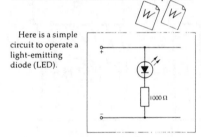

Here is a simple circuit to operate a light-emitting diode (LED).

This design shows the same circuit soldered on matrix board. The board is cheap and can be re-used.

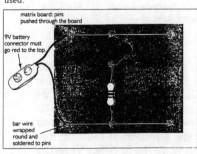

matrix board: pins pushed through the board

9V battery connector must go red to the top

bar wire wrapped round and soldered to pins

Transistors

collector

small current in

larger current

emitter

A transistor is a special semi-conductor. It has three connections: a base, a collector and an emitter. When a small current is put on the base, it lets a much larger current flow between the collector and the emitter. So a tiny current can control a much larger one.

● Try this water-detector circuit.

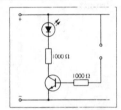

1000 Ω

1000 Ω

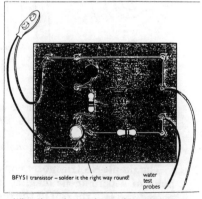

BFY51 transistor – solder it the right way round!   water test probes

When the probes touch something wet, a very small current goes from the battery through the water to the base of the transistor. This current is big enough to make the transistor work, so the LED lights up.

Figure 3 1991 Science text (Gott, Price & Thornley)

Again I have discussed these two texts elsewhere in somewhat more detail (Kress, 1998). Here I will simply make several quick points, to suggest the core of this issue.

- In the 1938 book, language is the central communicational mode. All the information which is to be communicated is given in the written text. In the 1991 book, language and image share the task of communication; some information is conveyed in the written language, some is converged in the image.

- As a consequence the relation of language and image has changed. In 1938 the role of (the quite few) images was that of 'illustration', that is, they reiterated information in visual form which had already been given in verbal form. In 1991 the images do not 'illustrate' the verbal text: they do not reiterate in visual form information (already) provided in the written text. Rather they provide complementary information which is *not* anywhere available in the written text.

- As further consequence, the communicational tasks of language and image have become specialised. In the examples here this specialisation means that the representation of events and actions (whether past, present, future, hypothetical) are provided in writing, and the representation of elements and of their relation are provided in the images. I have argued elsewhere that this may be characteristic of the new communicational and representational arrangements and that it may be more in line with the representational potentials of the mode of language-as-writing and that of the visual. (Kress, 1998, 1997)

- One consequence of this communicational specialisation is that as writing carries less and different information, syntactic complexity diminishes. I will discuss this briefly in section 3 of this paper.

- The social relations of the participants (author–reader; teacher–student) coded in the two texts are deeply different. This is realised in any number of features – in sentence forms (closer to speech-like language); in lexis; in use of syntactic features; in the terms of 'address' used; etc.

So my argument is that the representational world is different, and it is so because the world which is represented has changed. Social relations have changed, taking the science text-book pages as examples: school science at this level is now taught to a population which is no longer a small élite (as it was in 1938) but comprises all young people: the social (and gender) composition of the classroom is profoundly different. The 1938 textbook was written in an era in which the nation state was unchallenged; the 1991 textbook is written in the era of late modernity, when the nation state is under profound challenge. If the framings of values, of knowledge, of authority, of economic and social destinations had implicitly been provided by that state, in late modernity these framings have come under explicit challenge. If the nation state in 1938 saw itself as unproblematically monocultural (or if that question wasn't even a question then), then the same state in 1991 is culturally deeply plural.

To this must be added the vast changes in technologies of communication. These have produced a communicational landscape of a new kind: still with some recognisably similar features, and yet with features overall that make it significantly (and disturbingly) new. The effects of that technology have by no means yet played themselves out. The move from the *page* to the *screen* is a move from the dominance of writing to the dominance of the image. Once direct voice to screen interaction has become a reality (perhaps in a commercially viable form within the next two decades) the present relations of language-as-speech to language-as-writing will be unmade and remade in a manner that will change present conceptions of writing entirely.

Forms of writing (in *English*), at the moment, bear the traces or are the effects of a social, economic, technological and political history of about 500 years. When writing will have become, (with that new technology), speech displayed as graphic form on a screen, it will begin also to display the effects of the new social, economic, and political givens. Above all, speech displayed as graphic form on a screen, will develop in co-existence with image displayed on that screen – perhaps at times still reproduced as 'hard copy' on a page or even in a book!

There are two points to my small excursion here: one is to relate the present state (and the future development) of the communicational landscape to (the widest) social, economic, political factors – a mode of proceeding which is of course centrally that of those whose work is focused on 'events', and 'practices'. The other is to reflect on the use of the term literacy in this new arrangement. Literacy (a term in any case at the moment still confined to the English language, and to anglophone cultures) as a term grows out of the older social and cultural arrangements: its increasingly uneasy fit with the newer situation is perhaps best reflected in two trends: one is the now common pluralising of the term, as 'literacies' (and here it is an instance of the ubiquitous post-modern plural: knowledges, subjectivities, Marxisms, etc); and the unfettered metaphorical extension of the term into all domains of representation (and beyond): visual-, media-, computer-, mathematical-, business-, cultural-, emotional-, etc.

It may be that a term which developed in one era, with its social, economic, cultural, political arrangements, resulting in the dominance of one representational mode – language-as-writing, 'lettered representation', cannot readily cope in a new era with deeply different social, economic, cultural and political arrangements. It may be that the shift from public communication dominantly as writing to public communication in many modes, requires a rethinking not just of the term we use as the definitional term, but also requires a rethinking of the useful extent, 'the reach' of the theories which we have and use to describe particular phenomena. At the moment the term 'literacy' is used with an imperialising tendency, encompassing, covering, most forms of representation and communication. This has two problematic consequences: the theoretical, analytical and descriptive power of the term 'literacy' is more and more attenuated; and the modes of communication other than that of writing are not accessible to serious analysis and description.

Theory, to be useful, has to deal with the world as it is, and must stand in a real relation to that world. If the world of communication (and the widest environment in which communication happens) has changed and is changing, then the theory which deals with that world must be re-examined for its 'fit'. In my own area, that of education, of the school-curriculum, that is becoming an essential and unavoidable issue. The communicational demands of the societies into which children now in school will be moving extend beyond the demands for full competence in speech and writing. For the curriculum of communication to be at all adequate to those demands, and to the real needs of children, these questions need answers. For reasons of equity it is essential that newly discriminatory practices do not arise around the changed communicational demands and means of the present, and certainly of the immediate and mid-term future.

Literacy and/or Communication

If something real is happening to change the landscape of communication then we need precise questions, and we need clear answers. A whole new agenda of research opens out. Let me ask – not the precise questions – but some broad questions: Is it that we are simply using more representational means? More media/technologies of communication? Are texts simply becoming more reader friendly? or more entertaining? These questions aim in three directions: (i) the kind and characteristics of the representational means/modes and media of communication; (ii) the functions of these modes and media in this new landscape; and (iii) the social and cultural causes and consequences of these changes.

The first of these questions is specifically a question about distinctive potentials (and limits) of particular modes. What are these modes like? What can they do? What have they been developed to do in particular cultures? What effects do the different materialities of these modes have – in terms of what it is that can be shaped with them, and in terms of human bodily, physical interactions with them. It has to be said that while on the one hand such issues have been matters of concern over many (hundreds of) years in many different ways, whether in relation to painting, music, sculpture, theatre, film, or much more mundanely, in relation to gesture, space, clothing, and so on, on the other hand these concerns have been explored in the shadow of views of language as being the one full medium of communication (making the others marginal, in that sense) and/or without focus on a comparison with the potentials of language, and their relation with and to language. This sounds wilfully dismissive (or ignorant) of vast areas of work (for instance, in relation to the last question, the work of Roland Barthes in particular). Nevertheless, I believe that the new work to be done will need to be focused on semiotic modes *in their own right, in terms of their materiality,* and with a clear eye on the relative functions of all modes in the communicational ensemble.

The dual focus – on specific modes and their semiotic characteristics, and multi-modal focus on the ensemble of modes in communication and on their interaction – is in part the centre of my own work and that of others (see Kress & van Leeuwen, 1996; Kress, 1996, 1997; Lemke, 1998).

To go back to the Science textbook examples for one moment, it is possible to see the changes in cultural and communicational use of the mode of writing, and to speculate about the causes of this change in terms of the factors I mentioned above. Taking one paragraph of the 1938 textbook as an example, and a similar piece from the 1991 book as a comparison, there are stark contrasts.

> The simple electric motor consists of a coil pivoted between the poles of a permanent magnet (see Fig. 6). When a current is passed through the coil in the direction indicated in the figure we can show, by applying Fleming's left-hand rule, that the left-hand side of the coil will tend to move down and the right-hand side to move up.

The paragraph consists of two sentences. The first sentence has a structure of main clause, with a restrictive relative clause embedded to the complement nounphrase. The second sentence has a much more complex structure. The main clause, 'we can show that x', is modified by an adverbial clause of manner ('by applying …') and has as its complement nounphrase a co-ordinate clause structure 'the left-hand side of the coil will tend to move down and the right-hand side to move up'; each of the two clauses in that co-ordinate structure has an embedded clause structure: 'the coil will tend (the coils moves down)'. This sentence overall is modified by a complex clause structure, in which a 'head' clause is modified by a clause acting as an adverbial of place. Putting it simply, the first sentence of this paragraph consists of two clauses related by syntactic subordination; the second sentence consists (in my analysis) of eight clauses, in grammatical relations of syntactic embedding and of co-ordination – of parataxis and of hypotaxis. The structure of the nominals in the two sentences can themselves be analysed further – depending on one's preferred grammatical theory: 'the simple electric motor', 'a coil pivoted between the poles of [a permanent magnet]', 'the direction indicated in the figure', 'the left-hand side of the coil', etc. Some of these are likely to exist in this register as ready-made entities, that is, they are likely to be there as 'available lexis' – e.g. 'the simple electric motor', 'Fleming's left-hand rule' – and are therefore not produced by the writer as part of his making of his text.

The others, and the sentence-syntax, are the result of linguistic-cognitive work, work of enormous complexity by the writer. If you hold a realist view of text-making (as I do) you get an insight into the kinds of cognitive demands made by writing in this subject, and the kinds of cognitive processes which become habituated by writing and reading texts of this kind. In that era, becoming a scientist was as much about that as it was about knowing the curricular content of science (not that that could be separated from its representational form in any case).

Circuits

In your first circuits you used torch bulbs joined with wires. Modern electrical equipment uses the same basic ideas. But if you look inside a computer there are not many wires or torch bulbs. The wires and bulbs have been replaced by electronic devices like transistors, chips and light-emitting diodes.

The paragraph from the 1991 text consists of 50 words (61 for the 1938 example). It has four sentences; and six clauses overall. In the first sentence there is a relative clause; in the third sentence the relation between the two clauses is the paratactic 'if ... then' relation. There are complex nominals, as in the first example, 'torch bulbs joined with wires', 'modern electrical equipment'; but there are also many simple nominals 'computer', 'wires', 'bulbs'. This slight analysis and the simplistic statistics are nevertheless revealing: (the change at the level of the clause (up from 6.1 (in 1938) to 8.25 words per clause) is far less pronounced) and the number of clauses per sentence is dramatically different, from 5 (in 1938) to 1.5 (in 1991) per sentence. The lexis is simpler in 1991, as is the syntax. Passives occur in both examples, two in the 1991 text and three in the 1938 text; without doing any more overly simplistic counting, my impression is that in the 1938 text, the passive without agent is a dominant, foregrounded characteristic, its function being the well-recognised one (among others) of providing 'scientific impersonality'. In the 1991 text, the use of the personal pronouns 'you', 'your', as a form of address indicates that this is quite specifically no longer the intended function.

The social relations of the pedagogic environment have changed, and with it have come those deep changes in mode; and with them have come, in my view, deep changes in cognitive demands posed by the language. The first part of this statement is precisely the area where work on 'practices' and work on 'the stuff' of literacy come together, and need to come together. The second part of the statement is my unsubstantiated (and, I think, unsubstantiable) hypothesis. It bears, however, quite directly on the question of 'literacy or communication'. The usual assumption if and when such changes are happening is that writing is simpler, literacy levels have fallen, that there has, in that ugly contemporary phrase, been a 'dumbing down'. But here I want to put forward what I hope is a slightly more complex and plausible argument: namely that the change in the communicational landscape has shifted the location and the characteristics of the complexity, away from language alone, to the relation of language and image and of their respective semiotic functions.

In the 1938 example there is a reference to a figure '... a coil pivoted between the poles of a permanent magnet (see Figure 6)'. I have referred to this relation (following Barthes) as 'illustrative': language provides the information, as here: 'a coil pivoted between ...', and an image may then be used to repeat this information in visual form – to illustrate it. In the 1991 text the relation is entirely different. If you focus on the first diagram in the first column, and on its caption, you will see that the caption – the written language – is used to point to the image: its function is deictic; the information as to what an L.E.D. is, is in the diagram. 'Information' has been distributed between writing and image, the latter is not illustrative rather it is equally communicative. One kind of complexity has moved to the relation of language and image. Another has moved to the new task of 'reading' the image, as a fully communicative mode. And yet a further complexity has moved to the relation between the images. The first image in this column is related to the second (NOT as the text says as 'the same circuit') but in a relation of 'the realistically portrayed example' (the lower one – in the original it is in colour) to 'the highly abstracted version' of a circuit.

If the page is read using the traditional reading direction for a 'page', from top down, the reader comes to the abstract, general version first, and to the realist version after that. In school science *abstraction* continues to be the key to the 'real'.

But if we accept my (admittedly simplistic and insufficient) analysis here – even if only as a metaphor, we have come to a situation in which the discipline which deals with one mode – be it language or be it image – can not provide an adequate account of the textual object as a whole, of the message, nor of the function of each of the modes. The question is: do we extend the term 'literacy' to deal with the new communicational givens, or do we use a term such as 'communication' to deal with the new multimodal reality? My worry is that in continuing with the use of the term 'literacy' we will feel that – by and large – we have the means to account for the situation, and the means of accounting derive, of course, from language, when in fact we need to ask quite new questions about how images work, and ask them from the point of the image, and we need to ask, then, questions about the interactions of the modes.

In my view neither Applied Linguistics nor literacy can do its job unless we reframe the scope of their activity in this fundamental fashion.

In the kind of research in which I find myself engaged at the moment (an ESRC funded project 'The Rhetorics of the Science Classroom' – co-directed by Jon Ogborn and myself, with Carey Jewitt and Babis Tsatsarelis as the Research Officers) it seems clear that both in the way the subject is presented in textbooks and by the teacher, and in the way the subject is 'learned' and reproduced by the young people in classrooms, an absolute focus has to be kept on image, model, language, gesture, action. Information provided in image will reappear in language; a metaphor that appears in the teacher's explanation reappears as the shaping frame in a student's drawing (without any overt focus by either of the two on this); the shape of a physical model used in class affects the stages in a written narrative produced by students; and so on. Neither learning nor semiosis can be thought about by focus on a single mode. And in my opinion what happens in these classrooms (once one has begun to attend to this) is the case in all communication.

'Communicational Webs' and Literacy

We know that we use literacy for many purposes in many occasions. Whether we describe these as distinct literacies, or regard them as the constantly productive, transformative use of resources of representation is a question I won't put here. It is without doubt the area in which work on literacy practices has made the largest contribution. We are beginning to understand that we use distinct modes of representation and communication, with different media of dissemination. I think we have not yet developed a clear enough sense of the fact that we all exist in distinctive communicational webs, using both distinct modes and distinct media. The 10-year old with his focus on the playstation, its associated magazines, the material downloaded from the Internet, the novels which are beginning to feed off and mimic this phenomenon, the chat with his mates, this 10-year old is in a different communicational web to his sister who is more focused on books, on printed images, her own writing, games with her friends, chat of a very different kind. This is not the same concern as the documentation of literacy practices, I believe; it points towards understanding links of modes and purposes, of modes and knowledge, of media and potentials for action and interaction, and it points to larger questions of in-school and out-of-school practices, of out-of-school practices and 'the economy'.

The new communicational landscape, of multimodality (that is, representational means are multiple) in multimedia environments (that is, media of dissemination are multiple) demands a rethinking. It reconfigures the tasks of our work, whether in practices or in research, whether we (decide to) remain focused on a single mode ('Language is what *I'm* about') or whether we accept the givens of the new situation and of the larger frame. For me the new tasks, for everyone of us, are to understand the modes employed in public communication in their specificities, in their materialities, in their collocations with other modes and other materials, and in their relation to the media of dissemination. Of course, as always, there are choices to be made; our efforts are always limited.

Where do I want to put my effort? What is the extent of my theoretical interests? And where do I focus my practical efforts?

Work with language will remain essential; in my view it will need to be seen in its interrelations with other modes, and their potentials. Work in literacy will remain essential; in my view there is a crucial choice between an approach which stretches the term to cover all forms of semiotic action; or an approach which focuses on the particularities of the mode of lettered representation, with all its complexities.

So here you have my sense of a working agenda. I hope it connects in ways which can be productive with your own concerns.

References

Fairclough, N. (1989) *Language and Power.* London: Longman.
Fairclough, N. (1992) *Discourse and Social Change.* Cambridge: Polity Press.
Gott, R., Price, G. and Thornley, T. (1991) *Active Science 2.* London: Collins Educational.
Hodge, R. and Kress, G. R. (1979/1993) *Language as Ideology.* London: Routledge.
Kress, G. R. (1984/1989) *Linguistic Processes in Sociocultural Practices.* Geelong/Oxford: Deakin University Press/Oxford University Press.
Kress, G. R. (1996) Writing and learning to write. In Olson and Torrance (pp. 225–56) Oxford: Oxford University Press.
Kress, G. R. (1997) *Before Writing: Rethinking the paths to literacy.* London: Routledge.
Kress, G. R. (1998) A satellite view of language: some lessons from science classrooms. *Language Awareness* 7 (2 & 3), 69–89.
Kress, G. R. and van Leeuwen, T. (1996) *Reading Images: The grammar of graphic design.* London: Routledge.
Lakoff, G. and Johnson, M. (1980) *Metaphors We Live By.* Chicago: Chicago University Press.
Lemke, J. (1998) Multiplying meaning: Visual and verbal semiotics in scientific text. In Martin and Veel (eds).
McKenzie, A. E. (1938) *Magnetism and Electricity.* Cambridge: Cambridge University Press.
Martin, J. R. and Veel, R. (eds) (1998) *Reading Science.* London: Routledge.
Olson, D. R. (1995) *The World on Paper.* Cambridge: Cambridge University Press.
Olson, D. R. and Torrance, N. (1996) *The Handbook of Educational and Human Development.* Oxford: Blackwell.

11 Label Literacy: Factors affecting the understanding and assessment of baby food labels

GUY COOK and KIERAN O'HALLORAN
University of Reading

Abstract

This paper analyses the discourse of baby food labelling, firstly in general and secondly by considering in detail one particular label, and the problems which readers of it may have in separating information from persuasion. The work arises from a research project 'Design And Accessibility Of Baby food Labels From The Consumer's Point Of View' funded by the European Union (DG XXIV) which is running from autumn 1998 at six universities: Aålborg in Denmark, Gent in Belgium, Oulu in Finland, Reading in Britain, Stockholm in Sweden, and Santiago de Compostela in Spain. Its aim is to improve consumer protection by suggesting how important information on baby food labels can be made more accessible to consumers, and also to contribute to the harmonisation of labelling within the EU.

The project will take place in three stages. In the initial stage, we are creating a corpus of baby food labels in each of the six participating countries. This will enable us to describe both the language used, and its relation to paralinguistic choices such as layout, typography, pictures, and colouring. At the same time, we shall be undertaking a broader study of the communication chain of which the labels are a part, using ethnographic methods to collect information about the goals of the multiple senders of this genre (including manufacturers, distributors, nutritionists, copy writers, designers, regulators and legislators), and about the comprehension of labels by consumers. In a second stage we shall conduct a contrastive analysis of the texts, the factors influencing design, and consumer comprehension in the six participating countries. In the third and final stage we shall make recommendations concerning the presentation of information and how consumers can be educated to access it. The overall aim is to understand and improve 'label literacy'. We define this concept as the consumer's ability to select those labels and parts of labels relevant to their needs, to interpret wording to obtain needed information, and to assess critically the manufacturer's intentions.

Labelling: Social importance

Food labels are one of the most widely disseminated text types in contemporary society, seen by almost all individuals, including vulnerable groups of consumers such as children, the elderly, linguistic and ethnic minorities, people with low education and reading skills. Labels are also very numerous. More than 4600 new products came on to the UK market in 1996, and currently approximately 100 new labels appear each week.[1] In our project we have chosen to focus upon baby food labels, as a manageable sub-group in which accurate and accessible information is of particular significance. Just how important such information can be is illustrated in an international context by the continuing debate over the promotion of formula milk powder in poor countries. Without breast feeding, babies do not obtain the benefit of passive immunity passed on in their mother's milk. The risk of contracting serious diseases from bottle feeding is therefore increased, but it is further compounded when mothers do not have access to a clean water supply. Waterborne diseases fed straight to vulnerable babies causes what is now a common condition in many parts of the world – diarrhoea, vomiting, respiratory infections, malnutrition, dehydration and commonly death – known as Bottle Baby Disease. One pressure group estimates that a baby dies every thirty seconds from this condition.[2] Mothers who believe that the use of formula milk is desirable in itself, necessary when they themselves are undernourished, or when they have twins, can put their babies' lives at risk. In the rich world, these dangers are averted by clean water supplies, public education campaigns, and legislation on labelling. In Europe, for example, all formula milk powders carry information about sterile preparation and the superiority of breast milk. ('Breast milk is best for your baby' (SMA Wysoy); 'Le lait maternel est l'aliment idéal du nourrisson. Modilac Soja peut être utilisé si vous n'allaitez pas.' (Modilac Soja)). In a long running campaign, pressure groups have alleged that in marketing to poorer countries, some companies have either not made this information available, or that it has not been understood. Although this led to the 1981 WHO/UNICEF International Code of Breast Milk Substitutes, accepted by 118 countries, there is still considerable concern about the observation of this code.

In Europe a possible danger to infant health may be posed by certain concentrated fruit juices. It has been alleged in a series of legal actions that, if these juices are allowed to remain in the child's mouth for a long time (when given in a bottle with a teat or if the child's teeth are not cleaned afterwards), the sugar content (arising not from the addition of sugar but from the processing of intrinsic sugars in fruit) can lead to a condition called dental caries which causes permanent damage to teeth. Debate has revolved around whether such information and instructions such as the following made this danger clear:[3]

> DIRECTIONS: Shake before use. Always give Baby Ribena well diluted with at least 9 parts water. To keep bottle neck clean, wipe after use.
>
> IMPORTANT: Like all baby drinks, never use as a comforter (i.e. not for bottle-propping) nor with a dummy. Once a baby's teeth begin to come though serve in a trainer cup not through a teat.
>
> Do not leave your baby alone with any drink.
>
> Remember the importance of dental hygiene.
>
> NO ARTIFICIAL ADDITIVES
>
> Unlike some baby juices we add no artificial preservatives, colours, flavours or sweeteners. Ribena is super concentrated to preserve the product naturally.

While it is true that the risk of tooth decay would be minimised if carers followed the advice given, it may also be that readers will make a false inference based upon default assumptions in their schematic knowledge of baby care. The advice not to leave the baby alone, for example, might be interpreted as referring to some sudden danger which can be averted by the presence of the carer (such as choking or suffocation) rather than some longer term danger of tooth decay. Similarly, it might be thought that the juice should be given at meal times, or that water should be added, to make it more digestible, or tasty. The advice 'remember the importance of dental hygiene' can be reasonably interpreted as a statement of general relevance to all foods and drinks, rather than of particular relevance to concentrated fruit juice. Lastly the insistence that the ingredients are not 'artificial', and that nothing has been added, may suggest to those without technical knowledge of fruit processing, that no potentially harmful sugars are present in the product.

Labelling: Importance to discourse analysis

In addition to their social importance, food labels provide fertile material for discourse analysis, for a number of reasons. Firstly, in the contemporary world, discourse analysis increasingly needs to cope with both linguistic and paralinguistic communication (Kress & van Leeuwen, 1996), and labels, with their skilful integration of text with materials, colour, pictures, tables, and design, provide an interesting test case of its ability to do this. Secondly, food labels bring together within a very small space and short text, the interests of major discourse communities. On a food label, the discourses of business, marketing, aesthetics, law, science, health, environmentalism, and the family, all meet, intermingle, and compete. This can lead to apparently stark contrasts. While those parts of labels demanded by legislation, or giving scientific information, appear to be precise and factual, those parts motivated by the marketer's appeal to the consumer can be emotional, and/or extremely vague (Petré, 199). Persuasive strategies include making frequent use of modifiers such as 'natural', 'pure', 'healthy' (e.g. 'Oatbran is at the heart of healthy living'; 'Sensible eating and regular exercise mean a healthy lifestyle and a healthier you!'). As we shall see shortly, however, the separation, of factual and persuasive language on labels is by no means straightforward. Thirdly, food labels offer discourse analysis a concentrated range of different communicative functions. A typical label will contain instances of persuasion (referring to taste, health, environmental protection, value for money), warning (consumption date, allergenic properties), advice (for storage, cooking), exposition (ingredients, nutrients, guarantee) and so on. Like advertising, labels provide an interesting juxtaposition of discourse referring to matters of the most public and private concern (Cook, 1992: 136–37). It is the intention of the project to ascertain how easy or difficult it is for a wide selection of readers, of different backgrounds and levels of education, to disentangle all of these aspects of discourse.

Textual v Discoursal Meaning

Discourse analysis is the most appropriate method of analysis for accomplishing this goal, as it is both text-oriented and reader-oriented. In contrast to certain schools of semantics, which assess the truth value of each sentence in absolute terms, it studies systematically the principles by which texts are actually interpreted, by particular readers in particular contexts. As such it can show that conventional and reasonable understanding is based upon factors other than the truth of each sentence. From the standpoint of pragmatics, to which discourse analysis frequently appeals, a sentence may be literally true – yet it can be reliably predicted that a reasonable person will make a false inference from it. ('I have two children', for example, is literally true even if the speaker has six children, but will reasonably be interpreted to mean 'only two'.) Similarly, when a sentence is used in communication, its truth may be less important than its force or effect. Thus the same utterance 'This letter has to go today' might act as an order, a plea, or the refusal of an invitation, depending on who says it to whom in what circumstances. In addition, interpretation is influenced by discoursal features such as presentation, ordering and specific choices, and by background knowledge.

There is evidence that groups of consumers differ considerably in how they understand and evaluate information on labels (Múgica, 1990; Ringstedt, 1992; Glinert, 1997 and forthcoming). Often variations arise from differences in levels of literacy and education, or in command of the language. Morphy (1980) estimates that two million UK adults have difficulty in understanding information on food labels. Wright (1981) concluded that a substantial number of people often prefer not to read instructions. In his study, 48 literate adults were given a list of 60 products and asked how much of any accompanying instructional material they would read. In most product categories, instructions would be completely ignored on at least 30% of occasions; and for some products (e.g. fish fingers, hair spray, bicycles, kettles) over 60% of the informants said they had ignored instructions. There also appears to be cultural variation in the amount of attention paid to labels. A survey by COFACE (Confédération des Organisations Familiales de la Communauté Européenne) (1994) of 5000 consumers in six EU states found that while 93 % of the respondents claimed to read labels when purchasing, most of all the French and Belgians, only 20% of them could answer questions on labelling correctly, with considerable variation between nationalities (the French scoring 30%, Iberians 11% and Greeks just 2%). The disputes about both milk powder and concentrated fruit juices referred to above highlight the fallacy that the meaning resides in the text. In these cases, the issue at stake is clearly not only whether the necessary information appears on the label, but whether it is actually read, and, if so, how it is interpreted, by whom and in what circumstances. In the case of baby food labels, for example, reading is likely to take place in very distracting circumstances (shopping with a small child or preparing food for them) in which even an educated and well informed reader may fail to access, or misinterpret, important information. That labels should be designed to cope with such variations in readers and situations is an issue which needs to be addressed.

Both the law and the food industry, however, persist in the assumption that information is to be assessed in absolute terms, and thus fail to take reader variation into account. Producers are under pressure to harmonise labels and reduce costs, to distribute to wider international and increasingly diverse national markets, to cope with labelling regulations, and to contest law-suits. Although UK policy, following EU directives, advocates that food labels be 'easy to understand, legible and conspicuous' (Hunt 1995), it does not specify for whom, and in the event much product information is written and designed as though it were only to be read by mature, educated (even specialist) native speakers. As Kennedy (1991) puts it: 'The Anglo–US legal system presupposes what is essentially a mythical being: a legal subject who is coherent, rational and freely choosing'. By way of contrast, current German legislation on advertising builds in reader variation by ruling that 'an advert is misleading when it is shown that 10–15% of the targeted audience has been misled'.

Figure 1

NO ADDED SUGAR

100% ORGANIC

NO ADDITIVES

VEGETARIAN

MILK & LACTOSE FREE

NO INGREDIENTS FROM
GENETICALLY MODIFIED ORGANISMS

Carton made of cardboard
(100% recycled) and water based
varnish. Please recycle after use

ORGANIC INGREDIENTS

OAT FLAKES (53%)

APPLE (28%)

PEAR (19%)

INSTRUCTIONS

Place approximately 2 tablespoons (20g) of cereal into a bowl. Stir in 9 tablespoons (140ml) of baby's milk (breast or formula milk only) to desired consistency and leave to stand for 2 minutes. Always test temperature before serving. This is a guideline and should be tailored to suit your baby's individual needs.

A NOTE ABOUT GLUTEN

This product contains oats but does not contain wheat, barley or rye. Oats contain a protein which is similar to those in gluten which may affect some people who suffer from coeliac disease, a clinically diagnosed intolerance to gluten. For babies with no family history of coeliac disease, oats can be given from 4 months.

At Baby Organix we believe that nothing is more important than the health of your baby. So we have blended our babyfood recipes with only quality ingredients that are organic and natural.

Weaning introduces your baby to a world of exciting tastes, educating their tiny taste buds with foods that are suitable for their delicate digestive systems. Our Infant Cereals are specially prepared to be even easier to digest, and have a wonderfully smooth texture that babies love. We offer them to you and your baby as a way of helping to create a safer world, and a better environment with food you can trust. There is nothing artificial added, and the organic ingredients we use have been grown without the use of pesticides or chemical fertilizers. Studies have shown that very young children are especially vulnerable to these toxins.

We have lots of home made recipes and organic weaning ideas to send you. For these, or to share your suggestions or comments, please ring me on FREEPHONE 0800 30 35 11.

FOUNDER

Nutritional Analysis	Typical 100g of dry product provides	20g cereal made with 140mls formula milk provides	%of Daily Requirements* for a 4 month infant from made up cereal
Energy	1423kJ/335kcals	674kJ/160kcals	24%
Protein	6.9g	3.4g	27%
Carbohydrate	67.1g	23.6g	†
of which sugars	32.1g	16.6g	†
Fat	4.5g	5.8g	†
of which saturates	Trace	2.1g	†
Fibre	8.6g	1.7g	†
Sodium	0.01g	0.03g	†
Iron	2.4mg	1.56mg	26%
Calcium	45mg	71.1mg	18%

60%

† No Recommended Daily Allowance is set by the health authorities for these nutrients. * Recommended Daily Allowance

This product is sold by weight, not volume. Some settling of contents may have occurred during transport.

Figure 2

An Analysis of One Label: Baby Organix Cereal

In order to make the points above more concrete, the second part of this article is devoted to the analysis of one baby food label: Baby Organix Organic Oat Apple and Pear Infant Cereal. (Figure 1 shows the front, top, bottom and left side panels; figure 2 shows the back and right side panel of the label.) The purpose is to consider the relation between information and persuasion. In particular we shall pay attention to the nutritional analysis, set out in tabular form on the back of the packet. What is said here relates to one label only, and the analysis is taken from the project's preliminary work; examination of a larger corpus will help to identify the degree to which this particular label is typical or idiosyncratic.

At first sight, the contents of this label might seem to be easily divided between parts which are predominantly persuasive and those whose main function is to give information. Under the heading of persuasion we might include the picture of the healthy smiling baby which dominates the front of the packet. Here, visual suggestiveness is used in concert with language very effectively. The apple-green of the baby's t-shirt echoes the green of the fruit, and the packet's proclaimed 'green' concerns with nature and the environment; his healthy red cheeks matches the red sheen of the apples. The effect is reinforced by the text underneath 'HEALTHY BABIES', and, alongside the picture on the side of the packet, by his mother's endorsement confirming that this is a real baby who actually eats this cereal:

> Scott loves everything about Baby Organix, especially the taste and consistency. I like it too, because it makes him happy!

> Zeena Bishop, mother of Scott Bishop (pictured), aged 7 months.

Also overtly concerned with persuasion is the personal message from the founder of Baby Organix, Lizzie Vann, which occupies two thirds of the back of the packet. The message is personal and concerned in tone, addressed by 'we' to 'you'.

> At baby organix we believe that nothing is more important than the health of your baby. So we have blended our babyfood recipes with only quality ingredients that are organic and natural.

Sentences are laden with emotive pre-modifiers:

> Weaning introduces your baby to a world of exciting tastes, educating their tiny taste buds with foods that are suitable for their delicate digestive systems.

In this message the use of language is complemented by visual design and pictures. The font is one reminiscent of handwriting. The text is followed by a reproduction of the founder's signature, as though it were a letter or solemn undertaking, and to the right of this is a photograph of five smiling women (presumably the makers of the cereal). The oval shape and blurred edges lend this picture a somewhat old-fashioned character. The central woman (presumably Lizzie Vann), wearing an apron emblazoned with 'Baby Organix – healthy babies'. She is stirring a bowl of cereal and on either side of her there is a basket fruit and vegetables. The baskets in both front and back pictures are whicker. The connotative effect is of a homegrown (i.e. British), cottage industry, warm and natural.

Other parts of the packet contain more factual information. Thus we are told about the awards won by the cereal, its weight, the age for which it is suitable, the address of the manufacturers (in Dorset), the place of manufacture (Spain), the expiry date, the fact that the carton is made from recyclable materials, the ingredients, the resemblance of a protein in oats to gluten, the nutrients and their proportions, and that 'this product is sold by weight not volume. Some settling of contents may have occurred during transport'. There is also information for packers and distributors: a bar code and a label number. There are also directives. We are told how to prepare the cereal, asked to recycle the carton after use, warned (indirectly) not to eat the cereal if we have a family history of coeliac disease, and invited to contact the manufacturers. Given the simplicity of the product – it is after all only oat flakes, apples and pears – the amount of information and advice is extraordinary.

It is not the case of course that the separation between persuasion and information is so straightforward. Even the picture of the baby communicates information iconically about what is in the cereal and who it is for. It may be that many purchasers assess the product by the picture alone. In a similar way, parts of the label whose main function is apparently information also have a persuasive function. They are given varying prominence according to where and how they are positioned on the label. Bright greens and yellows, the contrast between light and dark, and larger type size are used to highlight the ingredients. Information about awards is foregrounded by the reproduction of badges on the top of the packet. The manufacturer's address in Dorset (a place with positive rural connotations for English consumers) is given much greater prominence than the fact that the cereal is made in Spain which is hidden away in small print on the bottom of the packet. The constant emphasis on organic produce and environmental concern ('All Baby Organix products support organic farming – the best method of farming to enhance the natural environment and promote sustainable soils.') support for the notion that this is a caring company. On one of the side panels, which are predominantly given over to information, there is a rather curious, a-grammatical string of noun phrases.

PURE FOODS

HEALTHY BABIES

A SAFER WORLD

While the absence of predication makes any logical interpretation of these phrases impossible, their parallelism seems to create a rather nebulous cause–effect relation. Language here is being used with a predominantly poetic rather than referential function; but the positioning of this phrase on a part of the label which is predominantly devoted to information helps to lend these phrases a more factual status.

Some readers are more vulnerable than others. We might suppose however that educated readers with a long experience of exposure to the persuasive techniques of advertising and marketing, might have developed a degree of label literacy which enables them to bypass those parts of the label devoted primarily to persuasion, and concentrate upon those factual parts which tell us what is actually in the packet, and which are tightly constrained by law. Readers of the BAAL proceedings may well consider themselves among this élite. On this particular label, these factual elements would be the mandatory list of ingredients, and the optional table of nutritional contents.

The list of ingredients does indeed inform us effectively and accurately of the contents of the packet. As the use of the term 'organic' is controlled, the informed consumer can also be confident that – as the founder's message also rather tautologically tells us –

There is nothing artificial added, and the organic ingredients we use have been grown without the use of pesticides or chemical fertilizers.

In the nutritional analysis we seem to encounter the factual discourse of science. Here are precise figures set out in tabular form. Any false information would be subject to regulation, and consequently (as is indeed the case) the information here is both precise and true. Yet even in this table, the communicative functions of persuasion and information can not be separated; the discourse of science is infiltrated by the that of marketing. The presentation may result in a number of facts escaping even a well informed reader. For example, in the left hand column which lists the nutrients present in the cereal we are told under the heading of 'fat' that there is a very low proportion of saturates, only a trace in the cereal itself. Many non-specialist readers, from their knowledge of the effects of saturates in adult diet, might suppose that this is a desirable feature of a baby diet. In fact, however, babies need saturates. (This is the reason that, in US legislation information about low saturate levels is not allowed on baby foods, on the grounds that it may mislead.) The second and third columns in the table, list respectively, the amount of each nutrient present in '100g of dry product', and in '20g of cereal made with 140 mls formula milk'. But why is the base weight different in the two columns? The effect, for an inattentive reader, is to suggest that the cereal is richer in nutrients, relative to the milk, than it actually is. The fourth column lists '% of Daily Requirements for a 4 month infant from made up cereal' and expresses these both numerically, and as a green bar showing iconically the percentage. The cut off point, illustrated by a dotted line on the right of the table, however, is 60% rather than 100%, thus making the proportion look greater. In addition this percentage figure relates to the made-up cereal (i.e. to the cereal and milk). An accurate interpretation of the second and third columns makes it clear that by far the greatest nutritional content is in the milk rather than the cereal. This table, in other words, though factually correct, is a good illustration of how presentation and reader variation as well as factual accuracy can affect the accessibility of information. It would be interesting to know how many highly educated readers who flatter themselves that they have selected this part of the label as the most reliable and factual, do actually read it correctly.

The above analyses gives present hypotheses based upon introspection into our own reading processes and purchasing experience. The aim of our project will be to check out these assumptions through investigation of more readers than ourselves, and more labels than one: to ascertain how labels are actually read by a variety of readers.

Labels and Applied Linguistics

Behind this project is a broader aspiration for applied linguistics. In the contemporary world, making information easily accessible is increasingly valued. Labelling is an instance of high profile public discourse of importance to the population at large. Members of the public need to select and access information, in order to safeguard their health, rights, prosperity, and general quality of life. With the interests of producers, regulators and consumers frequently at odds, enhanced awareness of the role of language is in the interests of all concerned. It is in an area such as this that applied linguistics can both contribute to the quality of life, and make its understanding of the use of language more widely accessible.

Acknowledgement

The authors wish to express their thanks to Professor Lewis Glinert, an associate of the project, for his help with this article.

Notes

1. Source: Campden and Chorley Wood Food Research Association.
2. McSpotlight on the Baby Milk Industry: http://www.enviroweb.org/mcspotlight-na/beyond/nestle.html.
3. The wording has now been changed.
4. From the volunteer panel of the Cambridge University Medical Research Applied Psychology Unit.

References

Cook, G. (1992) *The Discourse of Advertising*. London: Routledge.

COFACE (1994) *Family Consumption and Food Labelling*. Brussels: Confédération des Organisations Familiales de la Communauté Européenne.

Glinert ,L. (1997) Product safety information and language policy in an advanced Third World economy: The case of Israel. *Journal of Consumer Policy* 19(4), 411–38.

Glinert, L. (1998) Side effect warnings in British medical package inserts: A discourse analytical approach. *International Journal of Cognitive Ergonomics* 2 (1–2), 61–74.

Hunt, M. (1995) Labelling and legibility. *Feedback* 17.

Kalsher, M. J., Wogalter, M. S. and Gilbert, C. M. (1992) Connoted quantity of food-label modifier terms. In *Proceedings of the Human Factors Society 36th Annual Meeting 1992* (pp. 528–32).

Kennedy, R. (ed.) (1991) *Feminist Legal Theory: Readings in law and gender.* Boulder, Colorado: Westview Press.

Kress, G. and van Leeuwen, T. (1996) *Reading Images: The grammar of visual design.* London: Routledge.

Morphy, L. (1980) Information on food labels. In C. Riddington and D. Heighton (eds) *Understanding Labels: Problems for poor readers.* London: Adult Literacy Support Services Fund.

Múgica, S. C. (1990) Protection of the weak consumer under product liability rules. *Journal of Consumer Policy* 13, 299–309.

Petré, L. (1994) Safety information on dangerous products: Consumer assessment. *COFACE (Confédération des Organisations Familiales de la Communauté Européenne) Contact* September 1994, pp 6–7.

Ringstedt, N. (1992) Consumer safety policy in the EFTA countries. *Journal of Consumer Policy* 14, 413–29.

Wright, P. (1981) 'The instructions clearly state ... Can't people read?' *Applied Ergonomics* 12 (3), 131–41.

Notes on Contributors

Jill Bourne is Professor of Primary Education and a member of the Centre for Language in Education at the University of Southampton. She is Chair of BAAL (1997–2000) and Vice President of the International Applied Linguistics Association (AILA) (1996–99). She has researched and written mainly in the fields of language education and the raising of educational attainment in inner city schools.

Ulla Connor is professor of English and Director of the Indiana Center for Intercultural Communication at Indiana University in Indianapolis. A native of Finland, her research is on crosscultural communication and the teaching of writing across cultures in ESL and EFL settings. Her work has appeared in *Text, Applied Linguistics* and *TESOL Quarterly*. She is the author of *Contrastive Rhetoric: Crosscultural aspects of second language writing* (CUP, 1996).

Guy Cook is Professor of Applied Linguistics at the University of Reading. He began his career as an English teacher in Egypt, Italy, the UK and Russia, and worked subsequently at the University of Leeds and the London University Institute of Education. His publications include *Discourse* (OUP, 1989), *The Discourse of Advertising* (Routledge, 1992), *Discourse and Literature* (OUP, 1994), *Principle and Practice in Applied Linguistics* (with B. Seidlhofer) (OUP, 1995) and *Language Play, Language Learning* (OUP, in press).

Sheena Gardner is Lecturer in the Centre for English Language Teacher Education at the University of Warwick, where she teaches Systemic Linguistics, Discourse Analysis and Methodology. Her current research projects are in the areas of EAL assessment (with Pauline Rea-Dickins), taped oral feedback on MA assignments, and personal names in Botswana. She was previously Associate Professor in TESL with campus-wide responsibility for ESL at the University of Winnipeg. There she was editor of the *TESL Canada Journal*, and published in the areas of ESL adult literacy and educational change in the Czech Republic, amongst others.

John Gibbons is a Senior Lecturer in the Department of Linguistics, University of Sydney. He studies, teaches and researches Applied Linguistics. His research interests are language and the law, and bilingualism in many forms, including minority language maintenance, bilingual education, sociolinguistics and the social psychology of second language learning. He has published extensively on, and is personally committed to, the maintenance of minority languages. He has published many articles, and *Code Mixing and Code Choice – A Hong Kong Case Study* (Multilingual Matters, 1986), *Language and the Law* (Longman, 1994), and co-edited *Learning Keeping and Using Language* (Benjamins, 1990).

Sally Johnson is a lecturer in the Department of Linguistics at Lancaster University and researches mainly into language and society in the German-speaking countries. Her publications include *Gender, Group Identity and Variation in the Berlin Urban Vernacular* (Lang, 1995), *Language and Masculinity* (Blackwell, 1997 – co-edited with U. H. Meinhof) and *Exploring the German Language* (Arnold, 1998).

Paula Kalaja has a PhD degree from Georgetown University (US) and works as a senior researcher at the Department of English, University of Jyväskylä, Finland. She specialises in Applied Linguistics, including learning, teaching and testing of EFL.

Gunther Kress is Professor of English and Education at the Institute of Education, University of London. His publications include *Learning to Write* (Routledge, 1994), *Before Writing: Rethinking the paths to literacy* (Routledge, 1997) and *Reading Images* co-authored with Theo van Leeuwen (Routledge, 1996).

Theresa Lillis has worked as a teacher across a range of educational contexts – Secondary, Further Education, Adult Education and Higher Education. She completed a PhD in 1998 entitled 'Making meaning in academic writing'. She is currently working as a researcher/lecturer at Sheffield Hallam University and as a tutor with the Open University.

Kieran O'Halloran studied Philosophy/Social and Political Science at Fitzwilliam College, University of Cambridge. He worked as an English language teacher for three years and went on to complete an MA in Linguistics at the University of Essex. He is currently finishing a PhD in discourse analysis at the University of London Institute of Education. He is also a research fellow in the Department of Linguistic Science at the University of Reading.

Anne Pitkänen-Huhta works as a junior researcher at the Department of English, University of Jyväskylä, Finland. She is about to complete her PhD thesis on the construction of literacy in the EFL classroom. She is interested in foreign language learning, teaching and testing.

Pauline Rea-Dickins has recently moved to the Graduate School of Education, University of Bristol. Her main research interests are in language testing and assessment, and the evaluation of language education programmes. Her most recent book is *Managing Evaluation and Innovation in Language Teaching: Building bridges* co-edited with Kevin Germaine (Addison Wesley Longman, 1998).

Alison Sealey is a lecturer in English studies in the Institute of Education, University of Warwick. She is the author of *Learning About Language: Issues for primary teachers* (OUP, 1996) and has written a number of articles about policy and practice in the teaching of English language in the primary phase. She is currently completing a book, in Longman's 'Real Language' series, on children, language and the social world.

Brian Street did anthropological field work in Iran during the 1970s, from which he developed theoretical approaches to literacy in cross-cultural perspective. He taught Social Anthropology at Sussex University for over 20 years and is now Professor of Language in Education at King's College, London and Visiting Professor of Education at the University of Pennsylvania. Having worked and lectured in the USA, Australia and South Africa, amongst others, he is currently applying cross-cultural perspectives to educational issues around literacy and language in the UK.

Catherine Wallace is Senior Lecturer in Education at the Institute of Education where she has joint responsibility for the MA in TESOL. She is the author of *Learning to Read in a Multicultural Society: The social context of second language literacy* (Prentice Hall, 1986) and *Reading* (OUP, 1992) as well as a number of publications in the field of Critical Language Study.

Shirin Zubair is an Assistant Professor in the English Department at Bahauddin Zakariya University, Multan, Pakistan, where she teaches English Language and Literature. Currently, working for her PhD at Cardiff University, her research centres on culturally shaped beliefs and practices surrounding literacies in women's lives in underdeveloped, multilingual communities.